Quiet
Catalyst

Quiet Catalyst

The introvert's guide to thriving in your career

Sarah Manley

Re think

First published in Great Britain in 2024
by Rethink Press (www.rethinkpress.com)

For my mother, who has always believed I could

Contents

Introduction

A s I climbed the career ladder as a deep introvert, it was getting tougher. I was growing tired. I was increasingly berating myself. The feeling that I was in the wrong place was becoming overwhelming.

As a director in an international marketing role, I was 'always on', always visible – presenting, engaging, leading, networking. I felt huge pressure to impress with spontaneous supersmart comments in meetings, to keep pace with the after-work schmoozing at events and lead all kinds of fancy group workshops.

The content of the work was fine, and I loved the sector I was in. I was engaged and the business valued my contribution. The annual performance ratings and outward success looked great. Inwardly, however,

I was paddling mega hard. If I'm honest (and I will be in this book, so please be kind), this wasn't a new experience.

I had always found these types of skills challenging, although I had no idea why. It just felt that everyone else could do them and I couldn't; now I realise this is because these are skills that fall more naturally within the skillset typical of an extravert. Earlier in my career, I would dodge them as much as I possibly could. When I really couldn't escape them, I would grit my teeth, plaster on a fake smile so no one noticed my discomfort and push on through, then use all the downtime I had to lick my wounds from the ordeal, entering hibernation mode to recharge my batteries before going again.

While this approach kept me going day to day, by avoiding these situations and ignoring my issues, I'd never really learned how to manage them differently. It probably doesn't sound particularly fun or healthy – because it wasn't. I'm not sure how long this would have continued. I probably would have burnt out at some point, and when these skills became key to my job, all day, every day, things had to change.

A Christmas gift changed things. Two of my colleagues gave me a book. A plain looking and seemingly unremarkable book called *Quiet* by Susan Cain. I read it in one sitting and sobbed when I turned the last page – proper from-the-depth-of-my-belly sobs.

As an introvert, I'd found the whole book an absolute revelation. I was tired of faking extraversion and frustrated at the limited conception of the 'best way' to behave to be successful. Cain's assertion that 'In a world that prizes extraverts, it's OK to be an introvert. It's OK to be you' made me feel understood, that I was of value for just being me. I felt refreshed and ready to take on my challenges in corporate life with a new mindset. No longer seeing myself as in some way broken or inadequate, I now understood that I was amazing, and I was going to smash this!

The book you are reading is about what came next for me in learning how to use my introvert strengths as I advanced in my career, and finding greater ease in learning the skills that did not come so naturally. I can't deny that it has taken years of hard work and is something that I still work on today. Sometimes I have got it right and felt on top of the world, other times it has not been so great, and I have had periods of near burnout. This book is designed to help you find *your* way of being successful as an introvert in your career, and to show you some short cuts learned through the many hard-fought battles I endured in my journey of self-discovery and experimentation with how to be and how to lead as an authentic introvert.

Throughout this book, I will be using the terms 'introvert' and 'extravert' to refer to a person with a particular collection of personality traits. An introvert is a person whose personality is dominated by traits typical of introversion – a greater focus on the inner thoughts and ideas rather than external stimuli, and one who draws energy from alone time or time with just a few people. An extravert, or one whose personality is characterised by traits of extraversion, is one who thrives on the company and energy of others, seeking both stimulation and gratification from outside themselves rather than within. We shall explore this in more detail in Chapter Two. I recognise that I am much more of an introvert than I am an extravert, and this book is aimed primarily at those like me.

As many of the readers of this book will have experienced, in the bustling world of business, extraversion often takes centre stage. As introverts, we can find ourselves navigating uncomfortable waters and even find ourselves paddling upstream. We are the quiet thinkers, the unassuming problem solvers, and the reserved strategists, too often misunderstood and underappreciated, yet our unique qualities – when understood as superpowers and used to their full potential – can lead to huge success and personal fulfilment.

I'm writing this book because I've been there and done that; this book is the t-shirt. Over two decades, I built my successful marketing career in large international healthcare businesses. I loved the meaningful impact I could have through my work, but along the way I hit several bumps in the road. At first these felt insurmountable, yet eventually I found my way, and it's a path I want to illuminate for others. The world of work and business can be a demanding place, especially for those who possess the quieter strengths of an introvert. I've been through the highs and lows, the self-doubt and the triumphs, and it feels important for me to share the wisdom I've gained.

My vision is for introverts to enjoy excelling in their career, playing to their strengths and never feeling compelled to be shapeshifters or mimics of their extraverted counterparts to achieve success. I know the stress of trying to fit into a mould that doesn't fit; I found it utterly exhausting and unfulfilling. In this book I would like to share ways to find the right balance between using your introvert superpowers to their full potential, and finding new ways to enjoy building muscles for the skills that don't typically come naturally to us.

To succeed in the world of work, there are some unavoidable things that you are likely to find challenging – I'm sorry, but it's true. Situations like networking, presenting and taking questions, or speaking up in meetings cause many of us huge panic. It's OK, you are not alone. The good news is, if you want to build these skills, you 100% can. The even better news is that you can build them in a way that is going to help you feel more confident, manage your energy better, and even feel a bit proud of yourself.

When you have finished reading the book, I hope that I will have helped you to:

- Understand the value of introverts and *your* unique value

- Boost your confidence and energy

- Feel equipped and ready to practise new ways of tackling challenging situations

- Have the confidence to role model your introvert leadership behaviours for the benefit of others

During the process of writing this book it became clear that helping introverts to excel at work was a topic of interest to many different types of people. This is important to note because, although my intention is to address a specific audience (introverts) with one key message – that you can thrive in your career with the right know-how and mindset – there are opportunities for everyone to learn from my experiences. My aim in writing this book is for introverts to feel heard, valued, and supported in a way that is truly designed for their needs and preferences. Too often, we are overlooked.

That being said, I have to acknowledge that everyone is different. Everyone has their own unique set of experiences and capabilities. No one is purely an introvert or an extravert: we are all multidimensional. When using the simple terms of 'introvert' or 'extravert' to describe people, I will not be able to represent you or anyone else in your entirety – we are so much more than our labels. You might also find you don't agree with some of the things I say, especially when I am generalising for the sake of brevity, but I am never intending to offend or alienate. Our perceptions of the same thing will be different. That's OK. Bring that to the conversation.

How to use this book

This book is a comprehensive journey, divided into seven chapters and a conclusion, each focusing on a crucial aspect of thriving as an introvert in the world of work:

Chapter 1 – The Conundrum Of The Square Peg In A Round Hole: Here we will look at the common misconceptions about introverts and the challenges we often face. You'll learn about the enormous value introverts can bring to the workplace through understanding our amazing superpowers – after all, a square peg from another perspective is actually a diamond!

Chapter 2 – Your Introvert Fingerprint: This chapter dives deep into understanding introversion, helping you define your unique 'introvert fingerprint'. We will look at where your great strengths lie and consider where you may want to put some energy into building new skills to help you succeed.

Chapter 3 – (Re)Building Your Self-Belief And Confidence: Here we will discover strategies to (re) build confidence, shed limiting self-beliefs, and reframe negative feedback.

Chapter 4 – Energy Management For Introverts: Here we explore the power of managing your energy and using it to support you in achieving your goals.

Chapter 5 – Don't Fake It 'Til You Make It: This extended chapter is split into two parts. The first addresses difficult situations and scenarios; the second considers challenging interpersonal relations. In both sections, I share a wealth of practical strategies for succeeding in situations that many introverts find challenging, from networking to managing conflict. You can use your existing strengths and build new muscles to put these into practice from today!

Chapter 6 – Leading Teams As An Authentic Introvert: Contrary to outdated beliefs, introverts make great leaders, and in this chapter, we look at the important behaviours and tools you can leverage as you progress in your career.

Chapter 7 – The Future-Ready Introvert: Use what you have learned to role model future-fit behaviours to help you, and those around you, to thrive at work.

Conclusion – Putting Your Ideas Into Action: Reflect on what you are taking from this book and how you want to put things into action to thrive in your career.

I highly recommend that you capture your thoughts and actions in a journal or notebook as you go through this book. You will find exercises in each chapter to help embed your learnings and to start to put the things that are important to you into practice.

This book is for introverts who are feeling left out, overlooked, and frustrated at work. You have the determination and the talent, but you may lack a clear understanding of your innate superpowers and be unsure how to unlock new skills for career success. I firmly believe that you have the power, through a ripple effect, to have an impact on how introvert behaviours are perceived in business; you are taking your first steps by reading the book.

Together, we'll change the narrative of the world of work.

Let's do this!

QUESTIONS FOR REFLECTION

Before you dive into the chapters ahead, take a moment to reflect on the following questions in your notebook:

- What made you pick up this book?
- What, if anything, are you feeling concerned about right now in relation to your introversion at work?
- What would be your ideal outcome(s) from reading this book? How could this help you to be more successful in your career?

ONE

The Conundrum Of
The Square Peg In
A Round Hole

'In a gentle way, you can shake the world.'
— Mahatma Gandhi

Do you agree with this idea? At times it can be hard to imagine that it actually works. Although professional environments can vary greatly, I've typically found them to be loud, fast, and bold places where it is often felt that to get ahead you need to dominate conversations, network extensively, and maintain strong control over your team to deliver (and shout about) exceptional results.

When it's generally considered that 30–50% of the workforce is made up of introverts (Houston, 2019), it might surprise us that the status quo ended up this way.

In fiercely competitive and rapidly evolving companies, often marked by a constant demand for highly visible performance, extraverted behaviour is actively promoted. This approach is often perceived as instrumental to meeting ambitious targets, effectively interacting with both internal and external stakeholders, and assuming leadership roles. Typical situations in meetings, presentations, team events, and even impromptu sessions with the big boss dropping by seem to be the playground of the louder and bolder extraverts who thrive on being with groups of people, and the more people they have around them, the more energy they have. For introverts who prefer reflection, contemplation, and thinking before speaking, it can be easy to get overlooked and pushed aside. There are some common misconceptions that drive this.

Addressing some common misconceptions about introverts

Misconception number 1: Being quiet means you have nothing to contribute

Typically, an introvert will prefer to think carefully about their point before being ready to share it, and generally we will only add something when we are sure that it will add value to the discussion. This can have its drawbacks: sometimes the conversation has wound up and moved on before we are ready to add our contribution. The difficulty for us is that others in the room do not tend to be watching us or wondering what we are thinking but are usually just waiting for a suitable moment to add their point to the discussion; cue cutting in, talking over each other, and going round in circles. At times we may even find that we make a point that is glossed over, only to find that, frustratingly, someone louder makes the same point later and this time it is more positively received. All horribly de-energising to be part of and why we can often end up as a spectator in these scenarios.

In a world too often driven by overly fast-paced decision making, the ability to think through a scenario and weigh options thoroughly can be a game changer. Never underestimate the power of sitting in silence: it leads to more informed and considered choices, ultimately contributing to an organisation's success.

I remember once being in an important meeting in a new role, and I didn't say a word. I couldn't figure out what on earth to say that would be of any use, as the conversation flew all over the place, seemingly without a clear objective or direction. I left the meeting relieved to get out of there and desperate to retreat quickly to my desk and tackle my to-do list. A senior colleague, who left slightly later after connecting with the various stakeholders, was not happy. He told me, 'You cannot say nothing for an entire meeting and then just walk off!' I felt like I'd failed and was so frustrated, but now I realise that the fault was not all mine. We all have a valuable contribution to make, so let's find a way to ensure we make it *and* it is heard.

Misconception number 2: We are not good team players

It is true that we may enjoy independent work, often find ourselves on the edge of a group, and need alone time to recharge. It is not true, however, that we only work well in isolation. As introverts, we typically have great skills in listening, assimilating, interpreting, and manipulating data, deep thinking (going beyond the initial reactions, thoughts, and ideas), and solving complex issues. It's also important to remember that diversity in teams is critical to achieving the best possible results and avoiding groupthink.

The introversion–extraversion spectrum is just one of the many continuums of diversity that are important to have fairly represented in any high-performing group or team. Let's find a way to ensure we each have a clear and valued role within a team that plays to our strengths and provides support where we face challenges. Differences within a team should be celebrated for the richness they bring, and our introvert superpowers are proof of this.

Misconception number 3: Social awkwardness means we lack interpersonal skills

For most introverts, speaking in groups, whether in a formal or informal setting, tends to be a relatively uncomfortable and even disengaging experience, especially when it comes to small talk. All too easily the conversation can start to happen around us, and the longer we leave it to join in by saying something, the harder it gets to do so. There is hardly a second's pause to allow you to jump in, and by the time you've drawn breath, someone else has already filled the momentary gap. Exasperating!

Have you ever had that experience where you finally had a moment to add your thoughts and then stumbled over the words, or perhaps eventually got the opportunity to land your killer point, only for it to be met by a sea of bemused expressions and nervous smiles as you were too out of sync, too full-on, or too heavy for the conversation? You misjudged it, despite all that background thinking, and you walk away believing everyone thinks you're an idiot. The fact is that our greater strength lies not in these group settings, but in forming deep and meaningful relationships through one-to-one connections. Here we can really listen actively, ask insightful questions, and bring in our knowledge and experience at an appropriate level, giving more of ourselves and adding value to the other person.

Let's find a way to experience more of these meaningful one-to-one interactions while managing the bigger social settings in a way that enables us to feel confident and capable.

Misconception number 4:
Introverts can't lead others

What makes a good leader for you? A traditional (and I would say outdated) view of good leaders is that they need to be loud, bold, and able to give the rallying from the stage to motivate the workforce. There is a place for this type of person in all organisations, but there are also other ways to motivate teams and achieve visible results. In my experience, great leadership requires genuine relationships with team members, a coaching approach, and strong stakeholder management, especially in a hybrid working environment. In today's resource-scarce businesses, we typically have to wear multiple hats and deliver against numerous goals. It is key to be able to inspire, motivate, and empower our people to work autonomously, all while ensuring they feel fulfilled and engaged, if they are to stay in the business and remain driven and goal focused.

Guess what? Introverts can be great at doing these things! Our ability to form strong relationships, listen to and coach others, foster collaboration, and to think deeply and strategically sets us apart from the traditional leadership models.

During my research for the book, I spoke to a fellow introvert who had been asked to set up and lead a new team that was being carved out of a larger function. She was being deployed to a new country and faced a brand-new group of stakeholders. On her arrival, she was encouraged to be louder and bolder than felt comfortable to her. She disagreed. She had the confidence to say no, this was not her way, and she explained that she would remain true to her strengths and authentic style; after all, these were the skills that had gained her the new leadership position in the first place.

She decided on a new approach, one that felt genuine and natural. She began by conducting a 'listening tour' by speaking to each colleague and team member individually, to understand things from their point of view. This took time in the beginning but created a hugely strong trust and rapport that was invaluable in establishing herself and the new team, but also had an impact that lasted – sometime later, when the business faced significant major restructuring, hers was the only team from which no one left, such was the strength of the interpersonal relationships that she had developed. Her authentic introvert approach to leadership certainly proved its worth.

Like all stereotypes, these four ideas are misconceptions and far from the truth. Introverts, when enabled to embrace and leverage their unique strengths, not only excel personally, but can also have a huge positive impact on the dynamics and productivity of their teams and organisations.

Finding your fit

Introverts who tap into their strengths will likely experience higher levels of job satisfaction and engagement. Contrary to the common notion that introverts are unhappy in highly interactive environments, those that find (or create) an environment in which they can use their strengths authentically, while also effectively navigating the more extraverted moments, will not only succeed but will flourish.

Here are some pointers to help you identify companies that might offer you an environment that embraces your introversion:

- **Do your research:** Look into the company's culture, work environment, and values. Check out their website and social media pages. Seek reviews from current or former employees to get insights into whether the organisation values diversity of styles and behaviours. LinkedIn is a fantastic introvert-friendly way of reaching out to new people. Using it for the first time is scary but just go for it: connect with somebody in the potential organisation and send a short DM.

- **Build your connections:** Although introverts may find the idea of networking more challenging than extraverts do, creating links with people who can connect you to the right companies and roles is hugely valuable, and it's now much easier for introverts than ever before.

Start by attending (online) industry events or visiting digital forums that align with your interests. Building a small, close-knit network of like-minded individuals can help you discover opportunities and share valuable advice.

- **Embrace remote work:** Many introverts thrive in remote or flexible work environments. Remote work allows introverts to create a workspace that suits their needs, minimising distractions, and allowing them to focus on tasks. Look for companies that offer remote work or hybrid options if that aligns with your preferences.

- **Seek roles that leverage introvert strengths:** Introverts often excel in roles that require analytical thinking, problem solving, and independent work. Consider positions in any field where expertise and focused concentration are highly valued. You will probably find there are many more of these than you first think.

Introverts bring a rich tapestry of qualities and strengths to the world of work. Our innate preference for deep thinking, active listening, and empathy can have a transformative effect on teams and organisations. Recognising and appreciating these strengths not only leads to greater job satisfaction among introverts but also contributes to the creation of diverse, effective, and harmonious workplaces. In today's changing professional landscape, introverts have a distinct opportunity, and when enabled to thrive, we can demonstrate that quiet strength can speak volumes.

QUESTIONS FOR REFLECTION

Reflecting on what you have read in this chapter and your experiences at work, note down your answers to the following questions:

- What specific challenges have you encountered as an introvert in your career?
- How have these challenges affected your confidence and well-being?
- When have you been able to leverage your introvert strengths to the full?
- How could you find more opportunities to use these strengths?
- Think of a challenge you are currently facing. What steps could you take to address this? Think of one action and one mindset shift.

TWO
Your Introvert Fingerprint

'Be yourself. Everyone else is already taken.'
— Oscar Wilde

You are unique. Whatever labels you and others may use as a shorthand to describe you, you are as unique as your fingerprint. No two people are the same. Our differences are our strengths, and our shared understanding of those strengths is what can help us to thrive as individuals and in teams.

Introversion covers a continuum of personalities. What brings us together is the need for alone time to recharge. We get more of our energy from quiet downtime, as opposed to being with people in social situations. How much we need of that and exactly what that looks like varies between people, and across different moments in our life, just as our enjoyment of socialising and the more extraverted activities like team-building events or being in a crowd at a concert does.

I don't know about you, but I can really feel when I am 'peopled-out'. This is the moment when I know that the best thing I can do for myself is to head out on a walk or read a book in a cosy corner – but I could not live as a hermit either. I really value the energy I get from having positive people around me who can spark off a new idea or pull me out of a low mood. Like so many things in life it's about balance and knowing what a healthy balance looks like for you.

Remember that your introversion is just one part of you, and you are a rich, complex, and multifaceted individual. This is a huge area of possible exploration and potential value, and building an awareness of your unique introvert fingerprint can help you to better understand what makes you tick, your strengths and challenges, and your hopes and fears. In turn, this will help you to better navigate the professional environment with a confidence about why you behave in certain ways in particular situations, and some insights into how you could manage things differently to get the outcome you want.

In this book I will share how to get started in three key areas: your values, your motivators, and your definition of success. I have also signposted some further resources should you want to go further.

Your introvert fingerprint has four key elements:

1. Your introvert type

2. Your values

3. Your motivators

4. Your definition of success

This chapter will guide you through how to define your unique introvert fingerprint. I recommend that you set aside around twenty minutes for each of the four steps, although if you work through it more quickly or slowly, that's OK. The key is just to take your time and not rush. Sometimes what you learn about yourself through the process of going through an exercise is even more valuable than the result.

You can work through the steps in various ways. Bringing in different perspectives can really help you to build a rounded view of yourself but don't forget that the goal is to better understand you and your preferences. You want to start uncovering your own introvert superpowers to help you succeed in a way that feels authentic and fulfilling, so hold any labels lightly. Some ideas for how to approach this could include:

- Journaling
- Asking friends and family

- Asking colleagues

- Working with a mentor or coach

Remember that there are no correct answers. The only 'best' or 'right' outcome is the one that enables you to have identified your unique fingerprint. Be kind to yourself as you do this.

Defining your introvert fingerprint

1. Your introvert type

There are many ways in which introverts may experience and express introversion. Cheek, Grimes and Brown identify four types of introverts, according to their STAR model: social, thinking, anxious, and restrained. I have explained these and built on this list to include other types I have identified:

- **Social introverts** prefer smaller, more intimate social gatherings and find large, noisy events draining. They may have a few close friends and prefer meaningful one-on-one interactions.

- **Thinking introverts** are often deep thinkers and enjoy pondering complex ideas and concepts. They may be drawn to solitary, intellectual pursuits and prefer quiet, contemplative activities.

- **Anxious introverts** are more sensitive to social anxiety and may feel particularly uncomfortable in new or unfamiliar social situations. They may worry about judgement or negative evaluation from others.

- **Restrained introverts** are cautious and measured in their actions. They tend to think before they speak or act and may appear reserved. They value self-control and moderation.

- **Intuitive introverts** are often drawn to abstract thinking and may have a strong interest in future possibilities and innovative ideas. They enjoy contemplating and exploring the 'big picture'.

- **Empathetic introverts** are highly attuned to the emotions and needs of others. They may excel in roles that involve active listening, counselling, or offering support to those around them.

- **Sensing introverts** are highly attuned to their sensory experiences and may have a strong appreciation for aesthetics such as art, music, or nature. They may seek out and find solace in sensory-rich environments.

- **Ambiverts** are not strictly introverts, but instead exhibit a balanced mix of introverted and extraverted traits. They can adapt to various social situations and may feel comfortable recharging in both solitary and social settings.

Social Introverts
- Prefer smaller, more intimate social gatherings
- Find large, noisy events draining
- May have a few close friends
- Prefer meaningful one-to-one interactions

Thinking Introverts
- Often deep thinkers and enjoy pondering complex ideas and concepts
- May be drawn to solitary, intellectual pursuits and prefer quiet, contemplative activities

Anxious Introverts
- More susceptible to social anxiety
- May feel particularly uncomfortable in new or unfamiliar social situations
- May worry about judgement or negative evaluation from others

Restrained Introverts
- Cautious and measured in their actions
- Tend to think before they speak or act and may appear reserved
- Value self-control and moderation

Intuitive Introverts
- Are often drawn to abstract thinking
- May have a strong interest in future possibilities and innovative ideas
- Typically enjoy contemplating and exploring 'the big picture'

Empathetic Introverts
- Highly attuned to the emotions and needs of others
- May excel in roles that involve active listening, counselling, or offering support to those around them

Sensing Introverts
- Highly attuned to sensory experiences
- May have a strong appreciation for aesthetics, such as art, music, or nature
- May seek out and find solace in sensory-rich environments

Ambiverts
- Not strictly introverts but exhibit a mix of introverted and extroverted traits
- Can adapt to various social situations
- May feel comfortable in both solitary and social settings

You may feel affinity with one, more than one, or all of these. You may also find that it changes depending on your environment, your energy levels, and the stage in your life. Which of these most resonate with you now?

It's important to note that these categories are not rigid, and you should not feel defined or constrained by them. You may exhibit a combination of these traits and they may change over time, depending on the circumstances. The beauty is that everyone will have a unique blend of characteristics that make up their personality – their introvert fingerprint.

Whether you are strongly self-aware or just starting to think about your way of being and doing for the first time, it's helpful to engage in self-reflection and consider your preferences, tendencies, and feelings in different situations. Here are some points to think about.

- **Reflect on your social preferences:** Think about your comfort level in various social situations. How do you experience being alone? Do you enjoy small gatherings? Are you comfortable in larger crowds? Do you feel drained or energised after social interactions? Do you thrive in one-to-one conversations? Are you empathetic and tuned in to other people's emotions? Think about specific occasions, the context, and how it made you feel.

- **Consider your interests and passions:** What activities do you find most fulfilling? For example, are you drawn to intellectual pursuits, creative endeavours, or structured routines? Really think about what you enjoy doing. I encourage you to reflect on how this has changed; consider yourself at ages seven, fourteen, twenty-one, and in seven-year intervals up to today. What do you notice?

- **Seek self-knowledge:** There are lots of online self-assessment tools, and personality tests like the Myers-Briggs Type Indicator can provide insights into your personality traits, including introversion. Explore and find what resonates with you. Your workplace may also support various methods and trainings. Keep in mind that all of these tools and tests should ideally be used only as a starting point for your curiosity rather than to give you a definitive label.

2. Your values

Identifying and understanding our values is an important step in moving from surviving to thriving. Finding alignment between your values and the way you live your life can help with:

- Choosing a career, company, and role that bring a sense of purpose and satisfaction

- Staying true to yourself and finding an authentic way of being you, whatever the context

- Managing your overall well-being by understanding the clashes that will bring you tension and stress

- Finding clarity in your decision making, with the ability to align your choices to what really matters most to you

- Feeling fulfilled in life, at work and in general, by helping you communicate what is important to you, to set boundaries and live in a meaningful way

There are many tools and exercises online that can help you work through identifying and understanding the values that matter to you the most. I have included one exercise (adapted from *The Coach's Casebook* by Watts and Morgan), but I encourage you to explore what's out there and find what works for you.

EXERCISE: Defining your values

Below is a list of possible values. Divide a page in your notebook into two columns: 'Sounds like me' and 'Doesn't sound like me'. Then consider each of the values listed in turn and decide in which column to place them. Try to do it quickly and don't think too long about each one.

Feel free to add any values that you feel are missing from the list as you work through this exercise.

Looking at the list of values that sound like you, strike through those within that list that sound the *least* like you. Keep going until you are left with just five words. These will be the values that resonate with you the most.

Achievement	Fairness	Personal growth
Advancement	Freedom	
Balance	Friendship	Positivity
Challenge	Health	Power
Change	Helping others	Recognition
Community	Honesty	Reputation
Competence	Independence	Responsibility
Competition	Influencing others	Security
Co-operation		Service to society
Creativity	Inner harmony	
Decisiveness	Integrity	Stability
Democracy	Involvement	Status
Effectiveness	Knowledge	Timeliness
Efficiency	Loyalty	Wealth
Excellence	Mastery	Wisdom
Excitement	Nature	

I recommend that you keep a note of the key values you have identified and put it somewhere that you can reflect back frequently. When you are feeling successful and in your flow, look at the list of your key values and reflect on which are being supported by what you are doing now and by the environment around you. Similarly, when you are feeling stuck and frustrated, take a look and think about which values are in conflict with what is currently happening. This can help guide you into making positive and considered changes when required.

3. Your motivators

Understanding what motivates you is important to help you navigate what is driving you to set certain goals for yourself and to take certain decisions. It is especially helpful in moments of high challenge, stress, and low energy, when really knowing ourselves helps us to continue moving forwards and not to give up. This is going to be important to support you later in the book when we work to build new muscles for skills that don't come as naturally to us and push us out of our comfort zone.

EXERCISE: The five whys

This exercise is a great way to explore beneath the surface of what motivates you, and helps you identify the cause-and-effect of decisions. Here's how it works:

- Jot down three important decisions you have made in your current job role, and three goals that are important to you.
- Take your first decision. Ask yourself *why* you made this decision; write down your answer; this is the first *why*.

- Now ask yourself *why* the previous answer made you make this decision; write down your answer; this is the second *why*.

- Repeat the process five times, each time asking *why* to the previous answer, looking to dig deeper into the underlying reasons for your motivation behind the decision. Write down whatever comes to mind and don't be concerned if it doesn't sound exactly right. If you get stuck, don't panic. It is completely normal as we don't tend to think about our actions at such a deep level.

- Move on to the next decision, and then the third, before repeating the process with the three goals: *why* do you want to achieve this goal? *Why* is this the reason you want to achieve this goal?

- Reflect back on all the *whys* you have written. What themes are coming out? How are they making you feel? List all the motivators that have come up and rank them in order of importance with the most powerful driver first. Are you happy with the answers this exercise has exposed?

This exercise can be used to explore issues and identify motivators in all areas of your life, not just your career. It can be particularly useful to explore when things have not gone as expected, or to identify motivators that you many feel you want to change.

In a similar way to recording your values, I recommend that you keep a note of the motivators you have identified and save it somewhere that you can reflect back on frequently. Refer to them when you are facing situations where you are struggling to move forwards with an action or are confronted by a new skill you would like to develop. Think about how to reframe this struggle by selecting one of your motivators to help you.

4. Your definition of success

In the professional world, the conventional benchmarks of success typically revolve around climbing the career ladder, amassing wealth, expanding team size, and consistently boosting sales, thereby yielding greater returns for shareholders. This needs to change. In the post-pandemic era and amid escalating climate concerns, I believe that there is no more fitting moment to pause and reflect: what does success truly mean for me? Equally vital: what path do I wish to follow to attain it?

How you think about success is deeply personal, and its meaning can vary depending on your individual values, aspirations, and preferences. All are equally valid.

In this final part of this chapter, we will explore what success means to you in the context of your career as an introvert. By reflecting on your values, passions, and long-term goals, you can create a vision of success that aligns with your authentic self.

To define your vision, start by defining your success criteria. Consider how you are determining if and when something is a success in your day-to-day work. For example, is it about reaching a particular timed milestone, a numerical target, a financial reward, an expression of thanks, having a positive impact on another person, or something else? Often these metrics are predetermined by our company. Take a moment, though, to think about how you are evaluating success and achievement in yourself and in those around you. What kinds of criteria trigger you to think that someone else has done a really great job?

The next step is to set out your career goals and aspirations. Here you should aim to capture what you want to achieve and by when. You could set these along a timeline, or you could start with a word cloud of your ideas. Perhaps you already have a particular role that you want to aim for, but it could also be a specific company, or a defined impact you want to have. Personally, I have always struggled to know what role or company I wanted to set as a goal, so instead I focused on the impact I wanted to make and the experiences I wanted to have. Take whichever approach works for you.

Finally, write a vision statement capturing your answers and defining what a successful career looks like to you. Combine your personal and professional aspirations into a single coherent concept – this is your vision statement.

EXERCISE: Writing your vision statement

Use the following prompts to guide your thoughts to write a statement that you find meaningful:

- In your vision of a successful career, what kind of work are you doing to feel most fulfilled and engaged?
- What role or position are you in?
- How are you contributing to your organisation, industry, and/or community?
- What balance are you striking between your work and personal life?
- How does your success positively impact those around you, including colleagues, customers, and the world around you?

Here is an example of a fictional vision statement:
'In my successful career, I hold a leadership role where I have the opportunity to innovate and make a positive impact on the business but also inspire and support the growth of those around me. I am fulfilled by work that aligns with my values and passions, and I maintain a healthy work-life balance.'

Add as much meaningful detail as possible to your statement and put it in a place where you'll see it regularly. Use it as a source of motivation and guidance as you navigate your career, revisiting and refining it as you grow and your circumstances change, to make sure it accurately reflects your aspirations and what is important to you. Don't feel concerned if your idea of success does not align with the historical stereotype of professional success.

What if we could transform the status quo to be less about exerting power over others and more about fostering a collective of diverse and talented individuals to excel and feel fulfilled in what they do? What if success became about the positive impact we have on others as much as about financial growth? What a world that would be! More on this in the last chapter where we explore the role of introverts in the future of work.

You now have your introvert fingerprint mapped out. You have identified your introvert type, your key values and motivators, and defined what success means to you. You have developed a clearer understanding of what it means to be you and what is going to help drive you towards your definition of success. This is huge progress – take a moment to congratulate yourself.

I recognise that this chapter has posed some big questions and that the exercises take time to work through. Don't be put off if you find this challenging – getting to know yourself in this way can be difficult and may take practice. It can be hugely valuable to work through these exercises with a trusted thinking partner. This should be someone who will help you to think through what is important and reflect on what is really you. Your motivators, vision, and goals can change over time, so you may find it useful to revisit the fingerprint exercises at different points later in your career – for example, when starting a new role.

The good news is that, in my experience, introverts who invest in acquiring greater self-awareness and self-acceptance as part of their personal growth are more likely to thrive in their professional lives. When we truly understand and embrace our introverted nature, we can harness our strengths more effectively. This will lead to greater job satisfaction, enhanced performance, and overall improved career fulfilment.

QUESTIONS FOR REFLECTION

Consider the following questions as you reflect on what's come up for you during this chapter:

- What are your main takeouts from this chapter? Did anything surprise you?

- How will you use what you have learned about yourself in your current role or future career?

- What else are you curious to explore about yourself and how would you like to follow up on this?

THREE

(Re)Building Your Self-Belief And Confidence

'If you think you can do a thing or you think you can't do a thing, you're right'
— Henry Ford

I'm going to take a gamble and say that, if you are reading this book, you are currently sitting closer to the 'surviving' end of the professional spectrum than the 'thriving' end. When you've been existing here for a while, I'll bet your confidence is dented from uncomfortable events and feedback that has made you feel crappy. I get it. It sucks. As Maya Angelou observed in *Letter to My Daughter*, however, 'you can decide not to be reduced' by events outside your control: how we choose to respond to these knocks is in our own hands.

In this chapter we are going to look at techniques to build, or rebuild, your confidence, by understanding your superpowers (your strongest skills), and challenging your negative self-beliefs. It's important to have these foundations in place before we move to work on developing new skills later in the book. We will also be able to call on this newfound inner confidence and belief to keep moving forwards when things get tough and we are stretched out of our comfort zone.

The key to much of this work is to understand how to manage your energy to fuel you in a positive way. Trying to do new things that require high levels of confidence when you are low on energy is not going to set you up for success. Mastering your confidence, self-belief, and energy is going to unlock new possibilities for you. You've got this!

Understanding and boosting self-belief

What we believe about ourselves has a fundamental impact on the way we show up at work. Our positive self-beliefs have the potential to give us wings to do amazing things, while our negative self-beliefs act like brakes, limiting us and getting in the way of our performance.

How does it make you feel when you say positive things to yourself such as, 'I believe I am great at spotting patterns in data,' or 'I know I can take on this challenge as I've faced hard things before and succeeded'?

Do you want to do them? Can you see yourself enjoying them?

Funnily enough, these types of belief statements become self-fulfilling prophecies. You'll naturally lean into the stuff you believe you are good at, and in turn you will get even stronger and more confident at doing these things. Consequently, your self-belief also grows stronger, and over time, this even generates a great feeling of mastery.

To learn to thrive in a balanced way that unlocks our full potential, however, we also need to pay attention to what's happening with our negative self-beliefs. Just as the positive beliefs take a virtuous cycle, so the limiting beliefs take a negative downwards spiral. Consider what happens when you say negative things to yourself such as, 'I think that people don't warm to me,' or 'I know that I am awful at answering questions off the cuff.' How do you feel about these by comparison with the positive statements?

I'm sure you have experienced how one negative experience feeds into our existing belief that we cannot and so, in future, we don't. It becomes a defeatist cycle of not doing, not trying, fearing to attempt, not knowing how to… and around we go. Nothing changes, except the barrier just feels higher and more difficult to conquer each time. At best, we become known for being the quiet one, and at worst, the one who has nothing to contribute, is disengaged, or is awkward to approach. This is not the way to thrive. If you are wanting to thrive and deliver your true potential and impact, it's time to break this cycle. The good news is, it's absolutely in your control to do it, as this story from another previous colleague demonstrates:

'The mere thought of public speaking used to send me into serious "flight" mode. In the early days of my career, I could feel my legs receiving an adrenaline jolt strong enough to leap over the office walls if asked to speak, and it didn't get much better as I progressed.

'Every month, I would be sent an invitation to join a virtual meeting with our HQ colleagues and report on my brand's performance. I had never been one to speak up on the call – why would I? I knew I'd turn beetroot red, stumble over my words, *umm* and *errr* nonsense, and walk away feeling like a fool for not just a day, but a whole week – so I did my best to avoid the limelight of presenting at all costs.

'Sadly, there was a cost! You know what happened? The HQ slowly started to forget I was even there. I was gradually missed off distribution lists and eventually stopped receiving invitations altogether. It got to the point where I began to believe not only that I couldn't muster the courage to speak up, but that I had nothing of value to say anyway. The truth is, it became easier to hide than to try to participate.

'Everything changed when I finally had the opportunity to meet one of the HQ team leaders one-to-one. After we got past the initial awkwardness of them not even knowing I existed, they showed genuine interest in hearing my perspective on how the business was performing and my ideas for what could be done differently. That single interaction reignited my self-belief and made me realise that I could indeed contribute value to the company. It was a turning point, and I was ready to give it another shot.'

My colleague showed me just how powerful our self-belief can be. What stories are you telling yourself? How are these limiting what you believe you can and can't do? We all have self-beliefs that have emerged at different points in our life. Some might be valid, and some will have been created in our minds to protect ourselves from something difficult or threatening.

Let's start by identifying what you believe about yourself and how this is impacting you positively and negatively. From there we can tackle how to use the positive beliefs, and how to kick-out or reframe the negatives beliefs.

Here are several different exercises. Try them out and see which work for you.

EXERCISE: Future dreaming

Imagine an ideal scenario at work. It could be a future role you aspire to, a big deliverable you want to nail, or a piece of feedback you would love to receive from an important stakeholder.

Describe that situation to yourself and consider what you will need to do to achieve it, by answering the following questions:

- What are your key talents and capabilities that you will employ to get there?
- What else do you know you can bring to play to help you smash this goal?
- Conversely, what negative thoughts are coming up? How are these limiting or restricting you?
- Reflect on what this tells you about your self-beliefs. What patterns emerge in your helpful and constructive beliefs? What about in your more negative and limiting beliefs?

What, if anything, would you like to change?

Start to notice when thoughts about yourself and your abilities are coming up. Learning to be in the moment and noticing what is happening, what you are feeling, what you are thinking, and how you are reacting is a skill that takes some time to get comfortable with.

Your starting point is just noticing when you feel happy, light, and bright, or when you are feeling strong and accomplished. Also notice when you feel anxious, knotted, and uncomfortable, or over-whelmed and incapable. Ask yourself what's going on. Is it something that is actually happening in your environment or is it something that is happening in the way you are responding? Try not to judge yourself (not easy, I know), but just notice these thoughts and feelings and keep a note of patterns that come up over time. What are they telling you about what you are thinking about yourself and your capabilities?

EXERCISE: I am

- Write the phrase 'I am' at the top of a page.

- Now take three minutes to write down as many endings to this sentence as you can think of. Whatever comes to mind, go ahead and write it down. For example: I am smart; I am too anxious; I am the sort of person who shies away from conflict; I am the sort of person who cares about others.

- Next, mark with a green pen or smiley face those you think are positive things about yourself, and those that could help you to thrive at work.

- Now, with a red pen, or a non-smiley face, mark those you think are negative. These are the things that are holding you back from what you want to achieve.

- Look at your list and the distribution of the colours. Do you think this is a fair representation of who and what you are? Is it a helpful representation? Is there anything you'd like to change?

This is a powerful exercise to help you begin to identify deep-seated beliefs about yourself, and then decide which, if any, you would like to change.

How can we start to deal with the negative self-beliefs and the destructive impact they can have on our self-confidence and inner belief? The last two exercises have given you some tools to set you on your way to being able to name them, notice when and how they are showing up, and understand where they have come from. This is a big step so give yourself some kudos for that.

We will work together later in the book on steps we can take towards overcoming some of the self-limiting beliefs commonly held by introverts, and then consider how we can use these new abilities in challenging situations, such as presenting, networking, meetings, and so on. Like any skills, these are fine-tuned and honed with practice, but first we need to focus on how to manage the fears and restrictive self-beliefs holding you back.

We can spend chunks of our lives worrying about not being 'enough' – good enough, bold enough, visible enough. This feeling creates an unhealthy stress in our system which in turn makes it harder to develop and grow. By this point in the book, I'm sure you will be feeling clearer and more confident about the positive aspects of being an introvert, but I know that there will still be niggling voices in your head telling you that you can't, you will never be able to, you shouldn't try. Unfortunately I don't have a magic wand to make all the negative beliefs disappear, but there are ways to work through them.

Millions of thoughts pop into our heads every day. It is in your power to manage how you respond to them and how you allow them to make you feel. We are no longer going to let our negative thoughts about ourselves spiral and control us. You are in control. Ready?

EXERCISE: Reframe the negative

This exercise aims to help you identify and challenge your limiting self-beliefs.

Stop and breathe

Before getting swept up into a whirlwind of doubt and self-beating in the heat of the moment – stop. Breathe. This really is the first step. If you can stop yourself the moment a negative thought about yourself comes up, and just take a moment to notice it, you are half-way there. Now breathe. Breathing is always good.

Check in with curiosity

Just as you have started to do in the book, ask yourself some questions with curiosity to uncover what's going on. For example: where have you popped up from? What assumptions might I be making here? What would I be saying to a friend in this situation?

Reframe negative statements

Working on rephrasing the negative to a neutral or a positive belief or thought can feel more achievable than just throwing them out. Look back at your list of 'I am' statements you have written earlier in this chapter. Review the list and for each one that you have marked with a red pen or a sad face, ask yourself the following questions:

- How do I know that this is true?
- What was happening when I first started to believe this?
- What am I continuing to do that perpetuates this belief?
- What would a more helpful version of this belief look like?

Only by identifying these negative self-beliefs can we begin to challenge them.

The beliefs you hold about yourself are often formed early in life and early in our careers. Uncovering them and bringing them consciously to the surface takes courage and is sometimes quite confronting. As you start to understand them, you might recognise the negative beliefs as sore wounds arising from challenging experiences or even something far more traumatic. Both are legitimate. No matter where they have come from, the important thing is that you have recognised them and named them so that you are ready to deal with them. This level of thinking and reflection takes time. In the beginning it can feel forced and alien. Don't be put off. Over time it will become effortless, as you retrain your brain to spot these thoughts and seamlessly work through your checklist. Stick with it.

Keep in mind that you don't have to go it alone. There is a lot of support available to you. Discuss what comes up for you with trusted friends, family, or colleagues, and/or consider taking the topic to a coach. Most of all, be gentle with yourself along your journey as you work to uncover and manage these beliefs enabling you to progress in your goal to thrive at work.

Finding confidence in your superpowers

I am a big believer in focusing on our positive attributes and on our strengths. All too often we overlook these in a rush to correct what we are not so good at, or what we perceive we are not good at in comparison to others. This is doing yourself a huge disservice. There are so many positive things about you and your capabilities. Let's get it into our mindset to use them as superpowers!

For many of us, this might start with shifting your mindset about what it is to be an introvert. As young children, through school, and then in our careers, we will have developed clear notions about the 'best' ways to be and the 'right' ways to behave to be successful. Growing up in the Western world, or following a Western ideology, we will have learned that the preference is for extraverted behaviours, but this is not the norm in every culture. For those wanting to learn more about how the value and perception of introversion and extraversion differs across cultures, I can thoroughly recommend Erin Meyer's book, *The Culture Map*. Although these beliefs may feel entrenched, as we have already started to explore in this book, there is another way, and that way is your way.

To thrive in a sustainable way over time, you need to focus around 60–80% of your working hours on things that are fuelled by your superpowers. These are the things where you expend a relatively small amount of energy and receive lots in return. This returning energy can take many forms, including job satisfaction, a feeling of mastery, or positive comments from colleagues. By contrast, too much time spent 'shape-shifting' or flexing to behave in ways that are really not you is exhausting, so it is important to limit this as much as possible – more to come on this later. If 80% feels intimidating, remember that you already have a vast array of amazing skills in your toolbox and working with these will provide your organisation with enormous value, while also rewarding you with the energy and confidence to build on the solid foundations of what you are great at.

EXERCISE: The value of you

This exercise aims to help you recognise how your strengths have helped you achieve things in the past that had a positive impact on you and on others. By reflecting on your past achievements and contributions, you can gain a deeper understanding of how your introverted traits already positively impact your professional life.

Reflect on your strengths

Take a moment to write a list of your unique strengths, skills, and qualities that you believe you bring to the workplace. These can be both general and job-specific attributes. For instance, you might include qualities like active listening, attention to detail, empathy, critical thinking... Mark a star next to those that you consider to be your superpowers – those things that you are great at *and* give you energy.

If you've never thought about your strengths before, return to the introvert fingerprint exercises (Chapter Two) or the 'I Am' exercise from earlier in this chapter to prompt you. Don't feel awkward about asking colleagues or supervisors for input too. I can assure you that people will be delighted that you asked their opinion – see the section on feedback later in this chapter to help guide this process.

List your highlights and past achievements

Think back to specific instances in your career where your strengths played a pivotal role in your success. These could be situations where your identified superpowers directly contributed to your accomplishments.

Pinpoint your impact

Write down at least three examples of how your introverted qualities have benefited your teams or projects. These could be instances where your approach led to better decision making, enhanced team collaboration, or improved problem solving. Be specific in describing the contributions you made. For example, 'During a project review meeting, my ability to listen actively and consider various viewpoints helped the team identify a critical issue that we had initially overlooked. By addressing this issue early, we saved valuable time and resources.'

Summarise your value

Write down around five bullet points to summarise the value you bring to the workplace as an introvert. Include things like, 'I am an active listener who ensures that everyone's perspectives are considered, leading to well-informed decisions and cohesive team dynamics,' or, 'I have a talent for calming and focusing team members during high pressure situations, ensuring that projects stay on track and meet deadlines.'

Reflecting on your strengths, your impact, and your value can be a really empowering and powerful exercise, and one that it may be useful to look back on in moments of hesitancy or self-doubt.

At the end of this exercise you might be feeling really uncomfortable, really stuck, or perhaps really amazed at how valuable you really are. All are OK. As children, many of us are taught not to show off; we rarely get asked to think about our own strengths as superpowers and it can feel awkward. Knowing who you are and what makes you amazing is not immodest or boastful. It's about getting ready to share that value with the world.

Using feedback to build your confidence further

I really believe in the value of constructive feedback as a way of boosting someone's confidence by highlighting their strengths and supporting their growth. Done well, feedback can help us understand our blind spots and gives us fresh perspectives on our strengths and the areas we should work on. If this feels intimidating, remember that, unless we live as a hermit deep in the woods (an idea many of us would find highly attractive...), we are going to get people's feedback, advice, and opinions thrown at us from time to time whether we want them or not. I have always viewed feedback as a gift – that is, something the other person has picked out for you, hopefully with some thought and care, but it is your decision what you do with it once it's handed over to you.

There will be many points in our careers when we are encouraged to seek feedback, such as when entering leadership programs, when seeking promotion, or when gathering input for year-end reviews. This will often be in the form of 360-degree feedback questionnaires or similar, or sometimes delivered face-to-face. A feedback conversation can be extremely valuable when done well and with the intention of truly serving the person on the receiving end. Done badly, these interactions can be devastating. I have had some dreadful feedback at various points in my career that has really wobbled my confidence and self-belief. I am sure that you will recognise some of these examples: 'Sarah needs to be more impactful in meetings.' 'Sarah works hard and always delivers good work, but nobody notices or knows as she is not visible enough.' 'Sarah needs to be bolder and speak up more.'

Managing and filtering the feedback you receive is invaluable, both as a self-protection mechanism, but also to help you in identifying where you are working well and where you still need to improve. Be aware that all too often we find it is the sharp negative comments that stick with us rather than the supportive ones. Hanging on to these and allowing them to play on a loop in your head is likely to be damaging on your journey to thrive.

I have three recommendations to help you use feedback to grow, without it causing anxiety or adding to those self-limiting beliefs:

1. **Take feedback on your own terms.** Whenever possible, try to manage the feedback you are going to receive. One way of doing this is to ensure that you set the objective of the feedback, pick the questions, and select the people. I'd also strongly recommend that the feedback is requested in advance in writing, to give the responder time to think, and delivered face-to-face, so that they can hear the tone of voice, ask for examples or clarification, and ensure they fully understand the feedback. This means that you will get feedback on topics that are useful to you, with responses framed in a way that is constructive, and from people who really matter to you.

2. **Whatever comes back: filter, filter, filter.** This does not mean just throwing out what's hard to hear or, conversely, only focusing on the negative

and discarding the positive stuff. Keep an open mind and be receptive to different views. Look for patterns rather than outliers to get a better sense of the overall themes developing in the feedback. Look for anything that surprises you and consider what it might tell you that's new or different. Often you already know what will come back in feedback requests, so this surprising stuff is the gold – treat it with care. Do seek triangulation and confirmation to check if it is robust or just a throwaway comment written by someone at 5pm on a Friday. Think about your objective and goals and filter out anything irrelevant.

3. **You do not have to act on every piece of feedback you are given.** Draw a line between what is genuine constructive feedback and what is destructive to you. The destructive stuff you should throw in the bin and don't give it another thought. In my experience, feedback from someone will often inadvertently advise you to become more like them. Think about the people, their behaviour, and of the context of those giving the feedback and be selective about what you choose to follow up.

Overall, my suggestion would be to take two positive things and one thing that you want to work on from any feedback that you receive, always bearing in mind your goals. Let go of the rest.

Before we move forwards, I invite you to take a moment to pause. Look back at your work in this chapter and remember all the positive 'I am' statements, the amazing successes you've identified, and the greater understanding of yourself that you now have. Remember that you are enough; in fact, you are amazing. As you travel through this journey, you will grow into the spaces that are not yet comfortable. Be proud of your introversion and the qualities it brings that will help you on your way.

Progress takes time – but keep going. I believe in you, and you should too. Keep reflecting on what you have and who you are, and you will thrive.

QUESTIONS FOR REFLECTION

Thinking back to the points covered in this chapter, consider the following questions:

- On a scale of one to ten, ten being the highest, how would you rate your current level of self-confidence? Which elements of your confidence do you want to prioritise working on?

- What, if anything, surprised you about the exercise on your positive and limiting self-beliefs? Who could support you in reviewing or addressing any of these beliefs?

- How do you want to use feedback from others to support your confidence, self-belief, and career growth?

- Which five words would you use to describe your introvert superpowers – your greatest strengths – to a colleague, manager, or future employer?

FOUR

Energy Management For Introverts

'I still need more healthy rest in order to work at my best. My health is the main capital I have and I want to administer it intelligently.'
— Ernest Hemingway (cited in Baker, 2003)

B eing an introvert in the professional world can be pretty tiring, am I right? I am sure you will have experienced that feeling of being 'peopled-out' after a busy day of meetings, or you have suffered from a 'social hangover' from being in large groups. To perform at our best, where we can use our superpowers to the max, we need to consciously manage our energy balance.

Paying attention to your energy levels as an introvert in what is often a highly extraverted environment is vital to keeping on track on your path to thriving, and in ensuring you have enough energy left to enjoy your non-work time with friends and family, or just to be by ourselves without nose-diving onto the sofa! To help with this, it's important to learn how to read your personal energy battery level, and to learn when and how to recharge it. Understanding what affects our energy as introverts is important so that you have the energy to do the things that you love, as well as the things that you must do, while keeping yourself in balance. In this chapter we will look at the idea of the ideal energy balance for introverts, techniques you can use to recharge your batteries, and how to navigate the new focus on 'resilience'.

The introvert energy balance formula

Think of your phone. The more you use it, the faster the battery runs low. You plug it into an energy source and it recharges. We may be a little more complex than a phone, but the principle is the same for us. We don't have a percentage indicator on our foreheads; nor do we have a cable to recharge. But we can learn to gauge our energy levels on a regular basis and build into our lives recharge moments to ensure we are not hitting 'low power mode' before we realise it.

One way of doing this is to use the concept of the introvert energy balance. This simple formula is about getting the levels of energy coming in (the energy boosters) to equal, or even exceed, the energy going out (the energy drainers). This can be summarised as:

Energy boosters ≥ energy drainers
= Ideal introvert energy balance

Identifying and reframing energy drainers

While putting this book together, I asked fellow introverts what they found the most draining part of work. The unanimous answer was people! I think at this point it would be helpful to look a little deeper to understand what it is about spending time with people that can be so tiring.

The crux of it is quite simple: in social situations where you are putting more mental and emotional effort in than you are getting positive energy back out, your energy formula is out of balance, and you are left with a deficit. This is a common experience for introverts, but generally speaking, the opposite is true for extraverts: they get more energy out of social and group situations than they put in. Of course, this experience is not set in stone and different introvert types will experience this to a greater or lesser extent. It will also be variable over time: if your energy levels are already depleted, another social interaction is only going to drain you more, whereas if your battery is fully charged, you're more able to take the experience on without running into the red.

Doing things that drain your energy can be OK in short bursts, but too much expenditure over a long period of time results in empty batteries. Not only does this leave you feeling drained and exhausted, it also means you that won't have the energy to put behind the superpowers that you can usually rely on. This is what makes it so important to build your understanding of what specifically drains *your* energy and not to use broad generalisations. For example, in my experience it is rarely true that the drainer is *all people, in all situations, all of the time.* Generalising in this way can end up as another self-limiting belief. Instead we need to get specific and reframe the drainer to help manage the situation. For example, 'I don't like socialising at work' could be made more specific to become 'I don't like socialising in the bar after a meeting because I find it hard to be heard over everyone else and it's tiring to keep thinking on the spot in large groups.' This could then perhaps be expanded to include a mitigating energy booster: 'However, I do like the opportunity to talk to a few people one-to-one and in small groups on specific topics that interest me.'

There are always things at work that we feel conflicted about. We can see their benefits for our performance in our current role or for future career development, but we don't really want to do them because we don't feel competent, they knock our confidence, and drain our energy. You can choose to avoid them entirely, dodging them whenever they come up, but avoidance is only denying ourselves the acknowledged benefits. Let's find ways instead to deal with these things so that you can engage in them while feeling grounded, capable, and confident.

You might initially feel absolutely horrified that I'm not suggesting you just avoid these drainers, but building your skills in reflecting and reframing these challenges can help you to relax in the situation and lose less energy over time. Believe me, however intimidating these situations might seem, it's far worse to keep on beating yourself up, repeatedly telling yourself that you are no good at something and that you'll end up feeling like a fish out of water. That really is draining, and that inner voice is not your friend.

There is a way to confront these energy-draining activities in a manner that is true to you. You can find it and even come to enjoy using it, strengthening your skills as you do. Next time you find yourself worrying that something will drain you or leave you feeling less than competent, I invite you to reframe. Consider what you want to get from this opportunity. What value can you gain by giving it a go? Reframing a potentially negative or challenging experience as a personal opportunity is a hugely empowering mindset.

**EXERCISE: My Energy Balance Part 1 –
Identifying my boosters and drainers**

You may already have a good awareness of what gives you energy and what drains it. This exercise helps us to take a step back and look at the bigger picture both inside and outside of work.

- Begin by downloading the Energy Balance Part 1 worksheet from www.thequietcatalyst.com/book-downloads.

- Looking ahead at the next seven days, map out on the worksheet your key activities for the week. Include events such as meetings, presentations, deadlines, workshops, social events, rest, exercise, hobbies, etc.

- As you go through the week, take a few minutes at the end of each day to reflect on the day just gone. What happened to your energy as a result of each of your activities? Did it increase, decrease, or stay the same? Mark each activity with a +/-/0 to record how you felt.

- Add a note to summarise your overall experience of your day, and then indicate how it compared to the previous day: was it energy boosting/energy draining/energy maintaining?

- At the end of the week, look back and consider how your activities during the week have made you feel. What do you notice about your experience during the course of the week? How would you describe your energy balance for this week? Is it in credit or deficit? What, if anything, would you like to change for the future?

You should now have a good idea of how individual events affect your energy balance and how this impacts on you across each day and over the whole week. This information will be invaluable moving forwards.

Techniques to recharge and boost your energy

In my experience it is harder, and takes longer, to refill the first 50% of your battery than the second 50%. This makes letting your energy battery run down too low before looking to recharge counterproductive. While it can be tempting to keep going and going, driven by a sense that you need to keep up with others – don't. Be confident in setting your own boundaries and maintaining what *you* need to be healthy and successful in what you do. Don't leave it too long between recharges, and don't succumb to the pressure to overexert yourself with extraverted behaviours. Building a habit of little and often is typically a good way to maintain energy levels through the working week, sustained though revitalising habits or rituals every day.

Different things will boost energy for different people, but could include such things as reading a book, listening to a podcast, taking a walk, or having a coffee alone in a nice cafe. As an introvert, it is usually about finding quiet, reflective, alone time – but not always and not for everyone. Don't be defined by the intro-vert label. Try different things and use the previous exercise to reflect on how they make you feel and how they have impacted your energy.

The most valuable thing I have discovered is the importance of putting self-care on your to-do list. In our hyper-busy lives where success is too often measured by impact and performance (bigger, better, faster), there is a tendency to try to do everything, all the time, leaving nothing left to focus on our own needs. Planning time for you is important to ensure that your well-being and energy are not overlooked and to ensure you can maintain the right level of focus in your schedule. Finding small ways to do this as you go through your day helps to make this easier to achieve but just as beneficial.

In his book *Atomic Habits*, James Clear shares a technique called 'habit stacking'. This is a way of building new habits by integrating them into your existing routines. It involves pairing a new habit you want to establish with a habit you already do consistently. By linking the new habit to an existing one, you create a mental association that makes it easier to embed and adopt the new habit, quickly and easily building a chain of habits that become part of your daily routine.

What do you already do every day that you could pair with an energy-boosting habit? This includes things such as making tea in the morning, eating lunch, coffee breaks between meetings, watching TV, brushing your teeth before bed, and so on.

Having identified consistent and well-established routines, now consider what seemingly small things you could add to each of those habitual activities that would boost the energy in your battery. Examples could include taking a walk with your coffee between meetings, listening to a podcast over lunch, using a mindfulness app on the journey home from work, adding some gentle movements after brushing your teeth (a stretch to work out your kinks, five minutes of yoga to move the energy in your body), journaling before bed, reading some inspirational quotes before breakfast at the weekend, messaging a close friend twice a week, and so on. Not everything has to be a big action or a huge change. Don't let me stop you if that's what you want to do, but what we are aiming for here are small and sustainable things that will keep your energy battery topped up throughout your day.

To get started, I would suggest putting some structure in place. Motivation and enthusiasm are great, but you need discipline to stay on track. Here are some initial suggestions; try them out and find what works for you:

- Write down *what* you are going to do.

- Set a timetable of *when* you are going to do it.

- Nominate someone *who* you tell to keep you accountable.

- Decide *how* you are going to celebrate making new energy-boosting habits.

Over time, you will find that you begin to look forward to these boost-moments in your day. In the early days you may sometimes forget or question if it's working, but keep going, get straight back on the horse if you have slipped, and make adjustments if you need to. Have fun experimenting and learning about yourself. You may laugh, but what I have found really works for me is to use sticky stars to mark off my progress on a reward chart, just like a five-year-old!

Managing energy is both a science and an art. You can build structures and plan carefully, but sometimes stuff just happens in life, in work, in relationships. Having a toolkit to steady the boat helps. Sometimes you will find things are just 'off' and you're not sure why. Usually for me this is linked to lack of sleep, reduced physical activity, or when something is on my mind that I have not yet been able to articulate and it's buzzing around my head subconsciously. Keep listening, pausing, and reflecting, and you'll come to learn your triggers. Don't be tempted to copy-and-paste these from someone else. Learn, be inspired, and borrow ideas from them, but come to understand who you are and what balances your personal energy formula.

Preparing for intense moments

However well you are managing your energy on a day-to-day basis, there will always be things that come up in the diary that bring extra pressure, stress, or intensity. These will need additional preparation and careful energy management. It could be an interview, a pitch, or giving the first presentation in a new team. These are the things out of our comfort zone that will often leave us feeling anxious and wanting to run for the hills but try not to panic – it's OK, you've got this. Managing your energy to face them, and reframing the task to feel more in tune with your personal strengths will get you through it, and in time we will get you feeling stronger and more confident in these situations so that they feel less intimidating.

In these challenging moments, you want to be ready to go with finely honed skills, confidence, and self-belief. Remember that you have the knowledge, else you wouldn't be there, and you can do the content preparation – that's one of your strengths. Despite this, and however carefully we prepare in advance, much of our performance comes down to our energy on the day, at least in my experience: we want to be positive, rested, confident, and ready.

Movement, sleep, good nutrition, hydration, and doing what makes you feel happy in the days, hours, and minutes beforehand all make the difference to how you can show up. It sounds obvious but we don't always do it, often because we are busy running around, thinking about the event and everyone else, but not ourselves. Make a conscious decision to leave sufficient time for your preparation. Don't leave it to chance and get swept along by what is happening around you. Assign your personal preparation equal importance as your content preparation.

Tell people that you need 'your preparation time' and explain why it is important to you. A friend of mine recently told me that she was concerned about having to socialise with colleagues after a long flight before the following day's meeting. 'I won't be able to perform well in the meeting if I don't have rest and time to myself, but I don't want to seem like the recluse who doesn't want to join in,' she explained. My experience has taught me that it is always better to share with people how you are feeling and what you need. In doing so, I often find that there are others who are relieved by my honesty and then feel able to admit that they are feeling the same.

**EXERCISE: My Energy Balance Part 2 –
Planning and managing my energy balance**

This is a great exercise to use in a variety of situations. It provides a set of questions to help you think about your energy balance when you are preparing for something intense or embarking on something new, for example, a new role, a new training program, or a new project.

- Begin by downloading the My Energy Balance Part 2 worksheet from www.thequietcatalyst.com/book-downloads.

- As you did in Part 1, start by looking ahead at the next seven days and mapping out your key activities.

- Take a step back and look at the week ahead of you. How does it make you feel? What state of body and mind do you need to be in for what's ahead? Examples include rested, confident, positive, etc.

- Try to identify the energy drainers and energy boosters through the week.
- What does your overall daily and weekly energy balance look like?
- Do you need to plan more energy boosters into the schedule, and if so, where and how?
- Which are your energy drainers? Are there things you need to say no to in order to secure the time to prepare your energy as well as your content?
- What support might you need to make this week happen in the best way for you?

While this exercise is invaluable when faced by a particularly energy-intense challenge, it can also be usefully built into a regular practice on a monthly, weekly, or even daily basis.

While it can seem complicated to navigate your energy levels and how to keep them balanced, remember that you are not alone in figuring all of this out. It is highly likely that others around you are also struggling, but typically we don't tend to tell others what is going on for us so no one else knows and everyone assumes they are the only one. I can assure you that you are not the odd one out while everyone else is doing just fine, but what *will* make you stand out is your self-awareness and self-management. With these and the skills we are developing together, you can stay in control of your week while feeling confident and energised.

I do appreciate that this is a lot to think about and to put into action. When my energy is really low, and it feels a bit overwhelming to get started, I have a go-to question that helps me to take the first next step: what is the best thing that I can do for myself right now? I hope it helps you too. Another great resource that you can tap into is the work of Simon Alexander Ong – his book *Energize* can help you further explore the art and science of energy management.

Navigating resilience

'You need to be more resilient!' *Oof!*

Add this phrase to the ever-growing list of things the world tells us we need to be 'more of'. Too many people have told me that this has been thrown at them in their careers, and I have a real problem with it. With burnout at an all-time high, it would be remiss of me not to include a few words on this topic.

I will be honest; some people have said that 'resilience' does not fit in this book because it's not a skill specific to introverts. I feel that this is such an important aspect of thriving at work that if these words help just one other person, I don't mind. My intention is to bring an alternative perspective on resilience, to help you avoid getting swept along in the white-water rapids of company life, needing to grit your teeth to get through the day and attempting to balance it out with an office yoga break at lunchtime. The good news is that there is another way.

Resilience is defined by the *Oxford English Dictionary* as 'The quality or fact of being able to recover quickly or easily from, or resist being affected by, a misfortune, shock, illness, etc,' but, from what I've seen, the idea of what it is to be resilient has taken on different connotations in recent years. In our increasingly volatile and unpredictable world, where today's businesses are faced by a seemingly never-ending stream of difficult and bad situations, the notion of resilience (and 'bouncing back stronger') starts to feel loaded with judgement.

Resilience, in my experience and conversations in the corporate space, is associated with the idea of keeping going and digging in when things are tough, no matter what. It is the idea of gritting your teeth and keeping on delivering more, all while keeping a smile on your face. If we stumble, we are told that 'it's OK not to be OK', but the expectation is that we will pull ourselves together with an injection of self-care and get back to it ASAP.

That doesn't sound like resilience to me – it sounds like the road to burnout. One major cause of burnout is unmanaged workplace stress, generally related to the environment and systems in which we work. Watch out for signs of this. It is possible to be in the early stages of burnout for years without realising. Introverts are no more susceptible to burnout than anyone else, but as the number of burnout cases increases, it is important to bear it in mind when thinking about thriving at work. You need to include the ability to recognise, prevent, and manage burnout in your knowledge bank and toolbox so that you can help yourself and those around you. I have included some signposts to resources and sources of help on my website at www. thequietcatalyst.com/book-downloads.

I think we need to take an alternative perspective on how resilience in the workplace could look, and it is one which also leverages some introvert superpowers, including:

- **Staying calm in a crisis.** This is the ability to be fact-based and objective in difficult situations. You need to gather information, think through scenarios, but avoid catastrophising – catastrophes rarely happen. Just because our media is full of doom, gloom, and painful stories, does not mean that this is a fair representation of how the world is. Staying calm during a crisis is also about managing emotions and quietening your mind. This doesn't mean locking away your emotions, but instead recognising them as they come up. Write or journal about your experiences and/or speak about them with colleagues or friends. This leaves your mind free to think through things more clearly.

- **Staying hopeful and optimistic.** Know that difficult times don't last forever. This is not toxic positivity. It is not about covering up difficult situations and pretending everything is OK, or only looking on the bright side. It's about being open and honest with yourself and with others about the present state and your hopes for the future.

- **Calling it out.** As an introvert, you are probably famed for speaking when it counts and saying what matters. While louder people are shouting about the issue, the situation, and its impact, adding your calm, clear voice will cut through and make people stop and listen. Don't worry if you think your point has already been raised: just because someone else has said it (probably lost among a hundred other things), doesn't mean it landed. Speak up for what you believe in, whether it's about the way forwards, behaviours, or something else.

- **Giving space for a wobble and not beating yourself up if you crash.** We are all human, with rich, complex, and complicated lives and personalities. To appear perfect every day is simply masking what is going on beneath, to a greater or lesser extent. This will be easier on a good day when sleep, work, relationships etc are all in a good place and feeling under control. In a rough patch, things seem bigger and more intimidating because our brain is fighting a perceived threat. We start to feel stressed and anxious, and things may begin to wobble, feeling dangerously out of control. It might not be one big thing that finally provokes a crash, it can be many small/unnoticed things that build up over time. None seem significant in themselves, but together the feeling can be literally overwhelming. You may start to avoid harder situations, retreat from others, and feel a growing tension in your body that never relaxes. This is incredibly common and a normal response. Rest. Seek support. Never feel that you need to handle this alone. It will be OK and you will come out the other side.

QUESTIONS FOR REFLECTION

Take a few moments to reflect on the following questions about energy and resilience:

- What have you learned in this chapter about your energy givers and drainers?
- What might you need to change to manage your energy balance when facing challenging situations?
- What does resilience mean to you?
- How is resilience spoken about by your company and colleagues? What impact is this having on you?
- What behaviours and mindset around energy management and resilience do you want to foster in yourself and encourage in others?
- Who or what do you need to support you?

FIVE

Don't Fake It 'Til You Make It: Confidently Being Authentic To Thrive

'Nurture your mind with great thoughts, for you will never go any higher than you think.'
— Benjamin Disraeli

In this extended chapter, we will look at how to manage situations that introverts often find tough and uncomfortable. Don't hate me when I tell you that there is no magic wand – if it was that simple you would have figured it out already – but there are ways to reframe and reassess what you want to achieve and how you approach it in ways that play to your introvert superpowers, while building new muscles in areas that might not come so naturally to you.

This chapter is all about finding methods to manage challenges in ways that will feel authentic to you. It is split into two sections: the first addresses situations and settings that introverts may find particularly challenging, while the second half addresses potentially difficult interactions with others. Pretending to be someone you are not, even for short bursts, becomes exhausting over time and will not leave you feeling satisfied, so here I will share my experiences of what helped me. My invitation is to reflect on these experiences and use them to help establish your own way of doing and being that matches your unique introvert fingerprint. I really encourage you to lean into the things that challenge you. Look back to your vision statement from the fingerprint chapter and focus on what is most important to you. It requires some courage to get started.

Be disciplined about finding opportunities to practise the things that do not come easily to you. Like with any new skill, the more you do it, the easier it will get. It will also take grit to keep going. Don't be put off if things don't go the way you hoped straight away. Remind yourself why you are doing it and keep going. Remember also to take a moment every once in a while to stop and recognise what you are achieving along the way. So often we are focused on climbing the next mountain that we forget to acknowledge everything we have conquered so far. Look back periodically and celebrate your efforts. Paying attention to the good stuff along the way will really make the difference in creating positive momentum behind your efforts.

Challenges that introverts face

When researching this book, I found my fellow introverts were hugely forthcoming about the things they felt they were not so good at and the demands of their job that they struggled with. It was tough, but perhaps not surprising, to hear a long list of situations, scenarios, and challenges that people were finding overwhelming and frustrating on a regular basis. Look at some of the responses I received most frequently.

Look back at the exercise in the Introduction where you explored your motivations for reading this book. I expect that some, if not all, of your answers also came up in my survey. The list could feel overwhelming, but there are a few important steps you can take to steady yourself.

Recalibrate

When you are thinking about what you are not so good at, who or what are you comparing yourself to? We often compare ourselves to the strongest person we can think of, placing them on some kind of pedestal. For example, 'I wish I could present like this person from TEDx.' It's great to have an ambitious goal, but let's remember that this person has probably been professionally trained in presenting, has practised this twenty-minute session for months, and if recorded, their talk has probably been edited. What might be a more helpful and realistic benchmark or goal for you to take your next steps towards?

Reframe

Rather than try to navigate a big list all at once, think about the challenges as grouped together into some key themes that have common skills running through them. These themes will differ depending on your introvert fingerprint but here is an example of how the long list of challenges could be collated:

- Impromptu speaking

- Being with a lot of people for long periods

- Working with people who are not introverts

Reframing the long list into only three main topics helps us to put things into perspective and makes the whole subject feel more manageable. What common themes run through the list of skills that you would like to improve?

Reframing also makes it simpler to connect learnings from one situation and apply them to another. For example, being asked to speak about yourself in an icebreaker session is an example of impromptu speaking. You can carry over skills, techniques, knowledge, and experience for this to apply to other scenarios within the same topic, such as answering questions from the audience about your presentation.

You are also likely to find that you can use the same introvert superpowers within the themes you spot. Look at how three of your introvert superpowers can be used to tackle the key themes list:

Key theme	Introvert superpower
Impromptu speaking	Planning ahead
Being with a lot of people for long periods	Connecting deeply one-to-one
Working with people who are not introverts	Using listening skills

We will look at all of this more thoroughly in the course of this chapter.

Reprioritise

We might tend to try to tackle everything with the same intensity all at the same time. I find this especially true if I have received feedback that pokes at my introversion and has wobbled my confidence as a result. Ask yourself, what of this list is actually important? What makes it important for me *right now*? It's also important to be honest about the conditions that you need to thrive. Focus on what is in your control or in your sphere of influence and set aside the things that you cannot change. For example, consider how you can influence the way a meeting is set up to be more in tune with your preferences for reflecting before speaking. I also encourage you to tell others around you about your intention to focus on these new skills so that they understand what you are doing and what makes this important for you. This will enable them to support you as allies along the way.

Here are the top topics that many introverts often struggle with. Get curious about each one and remember to think about how you can use your existing superpowers as well as where you want to build new muscles to feel stronger and more confident.

Dealing with situations

In the first part of this chapter, I will address a number of scenarios most introverts find difficult. These situations and events can, of course, be avoided at all costs, but that is simply to survive. The aim of this book is to enable you to thrive, and to do so in a manner that is authentic and more comfortable to you.

Networking

The word 'networking' puts many of us into a state of panic. I get it. I can still find walking into a room full of people I don't know pretty overwhelming. To help me manage, I prepare and plan thoroughly – that's a strength I feel confident about using. One way I do this is by taking a few minutes beforehand to break it down into a plan of who I want to talk to, what I want to talk to them about, and for how long:

- **Set a goal**. What would you like to get out of this opportunity? Remember, if you're reading this book, 'Just to get through it' is no longer an acceptable answer – you can do so much more. To help with setting a goal, try reframing networking as simply 'having a conversation with people I am interested to learn from or share something with'.

- **Set yourself a time limit**. I like to set myself an exit time. I find that doing this helps to make the idea of an evening of networking and socialising feel less intimidating. Start with as brief a session as you need it to be to ensure you get yourself in there and practising it. You can then work to increase the time as you build your muscles and you have to expend less energy as the skill feels increasingly comfortable.

- **Set up space to reflect afterwards**, but whatever you do, do not give yourself a grilling. Would you do that to your children or friends? Probably not, so don't do it to yourself. As with other developmental areas where you are building a skill and confidence in tandem, to make your reflection constructive and valuable, I really recommend that you write down five things you did well – yes, five. These can be big or small – think back to the recalibration earlier to identify the most helpful benchmarks for you in your journey. Wrap up by asking yourself, 'What learning am I taking with me for next time?'

Now that you have an overall plan prepared, let's think about the mechanics of the conversations. Some of you may find this easier than others. Let me give you some tips for the opening and closing parts of the conversation that I know many introverts find especially nerve-wracking and awkward.

Walking up to someone can feel extremely intimidating. Start small: perhaps don't make the CEO the target of your first new forays into networking. Think about who you have already met, however briefly, and who you know something about and had a good spark with.

It can be good to have a standard intro on the tip of your tongue: 'Hi Mary. Good to see you.' It's great if you remember their name, but if not or your mind goes blank, don't worry and certainly don't let that stop you.

Help them to remember where they have seen you before: 'It's been a while since we were in that meeting together, discussing next year's plans.'

Show that you were listening to what they were talking about and that it resonated with you: 'I was really interested to learn more about your experience in pitching your ideas to the leadership team. Is that something you would share with me?' It is worth noting that asking for help is often a great way to get a positive response as your target is likely to feel flattered by your interest and the implied compliment.

What if the person you want to speak to is already chatting in a group? I know that the idea of interrupting and introducing yourself in front of onlookers is incredibly intimidating and will make you feel even more self-conscious. Remember that these kinds of social situations ebb and flow, that people move between groups and, most of all, that you are the only one analysing this conversation. No one will go home with your move to join the conversation at the top of their mind, no matter how clunky it felt to you.

A common concern that can prevent us from approaching someone for a conversation is the fear that we don't have anything to offer in return, especially if they are more senior or experienced than us. What could I possibly have of interest to them? Believe me, you have a lot to give. You do not need to have some kind of killer concept or breakthrough idea to be of interest, just listening and asking insightful questions is sufficient. People love to talk about themselves and to share their wisdom or guidance with those who seem genuinely interested.

Knowing how to close the conversation is also important. You don't want to be quizzing this person all evening or fade away awkwardly. Look for cues for when they have had enough: eyes looking around the room, glancing at their watch, changes in body language from intrigue at the questions to tiredness or frustration, and so on. Become skilled at spotting these subtle clues, and when you do, instead of trying to think of your next genius question, recognise that your conversation has run its course. This is not a failure, it is natural that these interactions end, so how do we close on a positive?

Start by showing appreciation, and that you have listened and valued what they have shared: 'Mary, thank you so much for talking to me about this. I really like your point about the importance of understanding what the leadership team wants to see in the pitch. That's something I will think about more.'

Leave it open to connect again the future: 'I expect that lots of other people are eager to connect with you. Thank you so much for your time. I hope we have an opportunity to speak again in the future.'

If networking feels scary, it's probably because it utilises several skills that do not come naturally to introverts, and you may have had bad experiences in the past. Now is the time to set those aside and move forwards with renewed confidence. You have the skills to network effectively and comfortably, you just need to keep practising.

Presenting

Presenting to an audience is probably one of the things introverts dislike the most. Being the centre of attention, feeling under pressure to speak perfectly and engage the audience can cause absolute panic in even the most level-headed among us. For me, presenting was always an intense experience, even as I built stronger capabilities and coping mechanisms to support me. What helped me the most was to think carefully about my preparation, and ensure I planned sufficient rest before and recovery after to keep my personal battery well charged (see Chapter Four on energy management for more on this). I have learned that, personally, it helps me to speak to someone – anyone – beforehand. This enables me to warm up my voice, laugh a little, and shake off some of the nervous energy. If I can combine this with some movement, especially a walk, this is even better and leaves me feeling ready to go.

There are several additional things that you can do to make presenting start to feel more comfortable and to grow your confidence. Don't be concerned if you aren't transformed after one try. Be brave, keep practising, and in time your efforts will pay off. It may be that presenting is never something you feel wholly comfortable with, but you are still on track to thrive so long as you are managing your effort consciously and managing your energy. Try out the following ideas and see what works for you:

- Take the pressure off yourself by reframing the task. Instead of thinking 'everyone is expecting me to give a great presentation,' how does it feel to reframe it as 'this is an opportunity to share my knowledge and ideas with others'?

- Avoid the temptation to tell your audience everything you know. You can sound more credible and have greater impact by crafting your message around three simple questions:
  - What do you want to achieve from your presentation?
  - What will add value for your audience?
  - What is your ask or call to action?

- Before you start writing your presentation and preparing the visual elements, begin by noting your key messages on pieces of paper or sticky notes. Move them around to configure and reconfigure the flow. Keep the key messages concise and limit yourself to only one point per sheet (and eventually one per slide, if relevant) to avoid them getting lost in the detail.

- Less is more when it comes to your slides. They should be designed as a visual aid for your audience, to ensure that attention is directed to your key messages, rather than as a script for you. Tailor the slides to what your audience needs to understand rather that what you need to get through the session.

- Avoid reading from a script as you'll quickly lose your audience. Instead, prepare your text carefully and practise delivering your presentation out loud.

- If it helps you, have to hand a printed sheet with three to five bullet points of key facts, names, or prompts. Sometimes just knowing that you have them there is enough to boost your confidence and removes the need to spend your energy on stressing about remembering them.

- Practise presenting in lower pressure environments as much as you can, to get used to hearing your presenter voice in the rehearsal space and in sessions with trusted colleagues.

- Prepare yourself in the minutes before so that you can start with confidence and feeling calm. Have someone on hand to sort out the technology so that it's not causing you additional stress. Connect with a few allies in the room before you get started – it's OK to let them know if you're feeling nervous. Sometimes just sharing that with someone can make you feel lighter and less intimidated.

- Plan your opening – get familiar and confident with your script. Start the presentation with something with which you feel comfortable. This could be an interesting fact or statistic, or perhaps an engaging story. This will set you off on a great start and give you a boost for the rest of the session.

- Plant one or two questions with people you trust. These can be on topics that you'd like to explore more deeply or perhaps points that didn't fit within the overall flow. The bonus is that they'll be asked in a friendly way, and you can have your answer prepared.

- Give yourself time to think when taking questions. Listen carefully to the question. Take a beat. Repeating back the headline of the question is a good way of confirming you have understood correctly, and simply saying thank you for the question before starting your answer gains a little bit more thinking time as well as engaging with the speaker. If you don't have an answer, don't be tempted to start talking and see how it goes. As introverts, we are rarely 'speak-to-think' people. Instead opt for something along the lines of, 'Thank you. That's a really good question. It's not something I've thought about from that angle,' or, 'I don't have those facts to hand,' followed by 'I'd like to take that away and come back to you with a clear answer.' Don't weaken your response by asking for permission, such as by tagging on a hurried, 'If that's OK…?' Just pause, wait for their nod of approval, and move to the next question.

- Slow down when speaking. It's tempting to rush to get the whole thing over and done with, but this is likely to end with you breathless and a bamboozled audience. Keeping your pace measured will help control your anxiety. Stand up to present whenever possible and pause between slides to let your message land. Remember the value in silence and leave space to allow both you and your audience to think.

- Plan how you want to close – don't be tempted just to trail off with relief at getting to the end. What do you want people to remember about the topic or about you? Think about how you want to feel at the end and what you need to do to achieve that.

- Ensure you are clear about the final message. Don't end with an open question, such as 'What do you think?' as this will invite questions from every possible angle. Instead try to direct your listeners and make clear what you want in return: 'I hope my presentation has clearly set out ABC; I would like your input on XYZ.' 'I would like your feedback on your readiness to finance this initiative. I'd now like to invite your questions on this.'

- My final recommendation is something that filled me with terror when it was first suggested to me but has had a huge benefit – taking a presentation skills course and being video recorded with feedback from the class. Terrifying to begin with, yes, but invaluable? Definitely. You'll be supported to dial up your strengths and be given specific tools to help you with things you need to improve. I dare you – go for it.

Leading workshops

Cue major anxiety in most introverts, but it's OK. Cut yourself some slack. Everyone gets performance anxiety. You can do this, and there are ways you can get more comfortable doing it and even begin to enjoy it with practice.

I am sure that we have all been in 'hot air' sessions where everyone seems to love the discussion and activity, but nothing actually happens as a result. The key to success is to have a diversity of inputs to get creative ideas, create an action plan, and get things in motion with everyone on board. As an introvert, we know how easily some individuals can get overlooked, but we also know that it is key to ensure everyone's voice is heard, all actively contributing, if we are to get the maximum impact from that meeting. This can feel like a lot of responsibility for those leading and can easily feel overwhelming, but remember two things: no one wants you to fail, and you don't have to do everything yourself.

Leading a session does not mean you have to be tap dancing solo at the front of the room the whole time. Play to your strengths. Your instant reaction might be to think, 'I have zero strengths when it comes to running a workshop or meeting!' Don't listen to these negative voices – I can tell you that's not true, and again remind you that you can use your introvert superpowers to help you. Here's how to break it down.

My recommendation is to start by noting down your answers to the following questions.

- What is the objective of the session?
- What would a successful outcome look like?
- What are the most important topics to cover during the session?
- What are the elements of the session that I am feeling confident about?
- What are the elements of the session to which I am not looking forward?

- How do I want to be seen and how do I want to feel in the session?

- What else is important to consider before, during, and after the event?

- Who or what can support me to achieve success?

You can now decide what you will do and how you will do it based on your strengths, the muscles you're learning to build, and the support you have around you.

To thrive you need to deliver *and* be known for doing it so be careful not to become the mysterious puppeteer behind the scenes: your position as leader should be immediately obvious, even when you are asking others to help facilitate. For example, you might decide to delegate the 'fun' icebreaker exercise, or the MC duties for the open Q&A session, but ensure you hold on to the opportunity to be seen to be leading. Bring in an agency or ask trusted colleagues to maintain the momentum through the day as your social batteries get depleted, but don't dodge the responsibilities just because they feel uncomfortable.

Most of all, lead by example and model behaviours. There is no need to fake extraversion, but instead show the way to include people who prefer a quieter style of contribution. For example, schedule time in the agenda for quiet reflection in brainstorming tasks, make space for sharing from those people you know need time to think before speaking, and plan down-time in the session for everyone, including you, to recharge.

Large group meetings

Much of what we have already covered, and the tips and techniques suggested, will support you in this setting, but there is some additional advice that I would like to share on getting your voice heard in large meetings.

Online meetings have really helped introverts speak up, through simple reaction and 'raise hand' emoticons, and with the chat box. It is important, however, not to rely solely on these quiet tools to convey your point of view; instead, ensure people hear your voice. For example, you could write a few words in the chat and then take the opportunity to come off mute and say, 'I'd like to expand on a point I made in the chat...' This approach gives you time to prepare, the space to think, and gives others a heads-up that you would like some airtime.

While this approach works well online, raising your hand before you speak is typically not the done thing when face-to-face. This does make it harder to get into the discussion as everyone is talking, talking, talking. 'If only they would pause for just one second,' we scream internally – so make one!

- **Use your body language:** Lean forwards and make eye contact with the person currently speaking.

- **Use your voice:** Key to getting your voice heard is just to start speaking. I recommend a short sentence that gets you in and started, for example, 'I'd like to add a point here.' Pause. Breathe. People generally will stop to hear from you as they'll know you are only speaking to add something of value.

- **Use your allies:** Share your struggles with your extraverted or more senior allies and ask them to help bring you into the discussion – 'Sarah, what's your view on this?'

Icebreakers

I'm not sure if any single word strikes greater fear in an introvert than 'icebreaker' – the surprise opportunity to introduce yourself in a supposedly fun and memorable way to strangers. *Shudder!*

First, take the pressure off yourself. You do not suddenly need to be a top comedian, a secret Olympian, or have some incredible celebrity story – you are enough.

Now that you can breathe again, I have two tips: preparation and deflection.

There are a limited number of variations on a theme that typically get asked as icebreakers so you can get a few ideas ready in advance. Remember that everyone else in the group will be only half-listening to you as they'll be too distracted by coming up with their own response, so don't overthink this.

In work environments, typical icebreaker questions usually aim to foster a sense of connection among team members by sharing something about yourself. Consider preparing some ideas to answer the following typical icebreakers – you can keep them stored as a note on your phone if it helps:

- Tell us one interesting thing about yourself that most people don't know.
- What do you enjoy doing outside of work to recharge?
- If you could have dinner with any historical figure, who would it be and why?
- If you were to describe your job in one sentence, how would you do it?
- Tell us about a book or podcast that you would recommend to others.

What if they ask a question I haven't prepared for? The good thing is it really does not matter. Answer the question you wish they'd asked. For example, you could answer an icebreaker question that asks for your 'all-time favourite band' with, 'I'm a bit stuck with this one as I really don't have a favourite band, but something I would like to share with the group is that I've just finished a great book about climate change that I'd really recommend to everyone.' Still interesting, still tells them something about yourself, job done. Be prepared that this may wobble a more junior facilitator, but don't sweat it. It's on them, not you. Also be ready for the new connections you're going to make during the break as people come to ask you about the great book that you've mentioned.

If impromptu speaking is your nemesis and you would like to learn techniques to feel more confident, I thoroughly recommend Matt Abraham's book, *Think Faster Talk Smarter*.

Team days

Team-building activities and away days, all apparently aimed at fostering creativity, communication, and collaboration – a nightmare for the quiet introverts. Let's cut to the chase: our experience on the day really depends on the team we're working with and how the day is going to be run. If it helps alleviate anxiety, consider asking for information about those two elements in advance.

Sometimes it can feel like a few colleagues view these sorts of days as their opportunity to be seen as the star of the show and buddy with the boss. Don't allow it to irritate you, although I know it will – it still annoys me. I'm human, not a saint, and so are you. Let them get on with it.

Put the day in perspective. It's one day. Don't feel bad if you don't enjoy it, but do make the extra effort to join in and get involved or you risk appearing negative and cynical. That's not a good look and not the way to thrive. Next time, consider asking to be involved in the organisation of the event. The introverts in the room will thank you as you gently push it in a more introvert-friendly direction, and you will have a focused and meaningful way of connecting with the boss and being recognised for your contribution.

Getting the most from your office days

Many people's working pattern is now divided, with one to three days in the office and two to four days working from home. My experience of shifting to a hybrid working pattern is that it revolutionised my ability to thrive at work and hugely enhanced my personal well-being. Having quiet downtime at home before work starts and through the day was a big shift from the hectic commute and noisy break-spaces, although sometimes this contrast made the office environment feel all the more amplified with noise and busyness. Added to this was a new sense of needing to be seen, and to be seen to be committed, during the time in the office. Hybrid working seemed to raise new problems as fast as it solved old ones.

My learnings for managing and getting the most from your office days include the following:

- Think about what you need to do to turn up in the best possible shape. For example, what needs to happen in your morning routine and on your commute to ensure you arrive with the right energy and mindset to enable you to use your time in the office in the most effective way?

- Be clear about why you are going in and what you want to achieve while you are there. If it's only because you have been told to you have to, it's always going to feel like it sucks. What is *your* reason?

- It may be that, during extended periods of working from home, you have formed some beliefs about yourself that feel cosy and comfortable. I invite you to question if they're still true. Thinking back to the typical misconceptions about introverts at the beginning of the book, consider how others could perceive your behaviour. The more you stay away from others and the office, the more cut-off you become and the harder it becomes to reconnect.

- Plan some quiet moments to recharge during the day. For example, forty-five-minute meetings can be just as effective as an hour. By scheduling things differently, you gain a quarter of an hour back to decompress, recharge, and get ready for what is coming next.

- I'd also advocate talking to other colleagues about their experiences of managing their office days. Remember, 30–50% of the workforce are fellow introverts and are likely to feel in the same boat as you. Talk to your extravert colleagues too. I think you will be surprised at how much you can learn from, and have to share with, people who have the opposite experience to you and struggle with the quiet of work from home days.

- Taking a moment just to stop and breathe or repeat a positive mantra really helps at times of overwhelm that may come up on these busy, pressurised office days. If overwhelm happens, you haven't failed – I can assure you that it happens to everyone from time to time. There are lots of mindfulness resources that can support you. Don't let any negative experiences put you off and retreat away from the office. Remember your objectives for going there and consider how they will support you to thrive in your career.

Travelling for work

This is something I did a lot of throughout my career. As a home-loving person who likes familiarity and ritual, travelling to unknown places or commuting across borders was rarely something I could imagine enjoying.

I once asked a previous colleague of mine how they managed an early Monday flight from Amsterdam to

London when faced with such a full-on day and week ahead. He told me he'd learned to be 'low energy' while travelling. I have carried this phrase with me ever since, and actively sought opportunities to reduce my energy expenditure in these situations to leave plenty for the working day.

Airports are unpleasant places, with bright artificial lights, booming announcements, and loud fellow travellers all contributing. This is where you have my full permission to turn inward and raise your defences. Ways to do this include using headphones with or without music, a cosy scarf or putting your collar up, finding a hidden corner to take your coffee away from the crowds, or even finding a quiet space in the multi-faith room. Find what you need and own it.

It's not only the environment that can be energy depleting for introverts, but also how we might choose to use the time. Resist the urge to start trawling through emails and messages to feel like you're making productive use of your airport time. The likelihood is that this will just leave you feeling overwhelmed. If there's anything you really need to pay attention to, pick out that one thing, deal with it, and close it down. If you want to use your time effectively, reading a book (fiction or nonfiction) is a great way of bringing some creativity and fresh thinking, or use half an hour to think about your week ahead, using some prompts to consider what you want to achieve, what you need to be successful, and how you will measure (and reward) your success. Being 'low energy' doesn't have to mean being unproductive – it just means making informed choices about how you are going to spend your time to best conserve your energy resources.

Dealing with others

We have covered several settings, events, and scenarios that can be particularly problematic for introverts, and I have outlined a number of tips and techniques that I have found useful. We now move our attention to the sort of issues and challenging situations that can occur from our interactions with others. Meeting, engaging, and interacting with others is not optional. Managing these exchanges successfully is the key to thriving in the workplace.

Working with an extraverted boss

At times we all need to work with a line manager who has a different way of thinking and acting from ours. The advice I give here can be used with anyone who operates differently from you, whether they are an extravert or just have different preferences in working style. It can also be applied to colleagues at all levels, not only to those holding positions above you, as it is almost always possible to find common ground and work effectively together. Open and ongoing communication is vital.

Every story has two sides. It's important to think not only about why you might be finding the relationship difficult, but also to look from their perspective and consider why your boss might be getting frustrated with the situation. In general, I've noticed that introverts can find the boss's outgoing nature overwhelming and can feel under pressure to engage in more social interactions than they're comfortable with. On the other hand, an extraverted boss sometimes perceives the introverted employee as too reserved or disengaged, and potentially overlooks their quiet yet valuable contributions.

Understanding and navigating these differences in styles is crucial for a balanced working relationship where you can both thrive. When under stress, these differences are put into a pressure cooker and can easily escalate, leading to friction and even a breakdown of the relationship. All too often, we rush to jump into business topics with our boss – to share status updates, get alignment, or prepare for the next meeting. I have learned, however, that in any working relationship – and especially with your boss – it's imperative to have an initial conversation about ways of working to understand what it is that you both need to thrive in your roles. Once you both understand each other's expectations and needs, working life becomes a lot simpler.

By assessing your introvert fingerprint earlier in the book, you will have developed a good understanding of what makes you tick, your superpowers, and what you need to put in place to thrive. Setting up a conversation with your boss to discuss this may seem daunting and unnatural but it can be worth its weight in gold. A great time to do it could be in an end-of-year conversation about your performance, or in a personal development plan session, but honestly, in my experience, there's no time like the present. The sooner you have the discussion, the sooner you can start to reap the benefits.

When you're going into this conversation, there are a couple of things to bear in mind:

- What do you want to change as a result of the conversation?
- What is the likely reaction of your boss?

You could think of this as a negotiation. You're going to ask for something and they're either going to give it to you, or potentially offer something else in return. Would anything else be acceptable to you? Try to keep an open mind. Be ready to discuss what makes this important for you and to explain the positive difference it will make to them too.

Influencing stakeholders

This sounds like the title of at least one training course I've attended. The ability to exert influence and/or impact is a highly valued skill that is increasingly required in work at all levels, but especially in higher managerial roles.

Exerting influence is about selling ideas and proposals, convincing others to get on your train and to become active proponents of your view and direction. Having an impact is about two things: having the gravitas to make a lasting impression in every interaction, and achieving measurable results, shifting the needle from A to B, driving growth, or delivering a measure of success.

On face value, these qualities look like the typical stomping ground of extraverts: behaviours most easily manifest in networking, actively pushing and shaping, being bold and strong about what they've achieved, and making sure to let everyone know about it. As an introvert, I felt a lot of frustration at feedback suggesting I needed to have more impact or a stronger influence. Once again, this felt like I was effectively being told to be louder, more dominant, and more like my extraverted colleagues. I felt sure that couldn't be the only way, and it turned out that I was right.

I think it is true that to move things forwards in most large organisations we need to find ways to go beyond simply sharing our ideas within the company, to move on to selling them to the right people with strong storytelling and solid conviction. There are, however, ways to influence the stakeholders to buy into your ideas, and to impact the organisation, through your behaviour and your results, in a way that is truly authentic, sometimes an even more impactful way! We shall explore some of those here.

EXERCISE: Map your stakeholders

When approaching your goals and projects, it is important to think proactively about who you need to convince, to get input from, and to inform along the way. As an introvert, it is tempting to keep your head down, produce what you think is a wonderful piece of work and present it in a *ta-dah* moment. Unfortunately, most people don't like these kinds of surprises. You will miss out on valuable additions from others, and you may not get the recognition you deserve for all the work you have put in. Instead, use your deep-connection superpowers to engage people along the way, to gather their input, and smooth the path. A great way to start is to map out the relevant stakeholders and the quality of your relationship with them, using the following steps:

- First, download the Map Your Stakeholders worksheet from www.thequietcatalyst.com/book-downloads.

- Think of a particular goal you want to achieve. This can be anything from securing your next promotion to delivering a successful presentation to the leadership team.

- Note down all the stakeholders around you that could support or hinder your progress towards this goal.

- Next, map your relationship with each of them in turn by drawing connecting lines, using a simple key: two solid lines to indicate a strongly supportive relationship, one solid line for a positive connection, a dotted line for connected but neutral, a wiggly line for a weak relationship, or no line for no relationship yet.

Understanding the nature of your relationship with these important groups of people can help you identify where you can expect support, where to find easy interactions, and where you may need to put in additional effort to build a positive and supportive relationship. This information can help you manage your efforts – and your energy – more effectively.

Having an impact

Now you have considered who you need to influence, let's think about how you can use your gravitas to increase your impact.

Gravitas can be understood as having a certain weight of authority in our manner, and the ability to inspire positive feelings such as trust and respect in others. As quiet and perhaps unassuming introverts, we can sometimes risk disappearing into the wallpaper, and the more we shrink back, the less opportunity we give ourselves to have an impact. We may have a complex and fascinating inner dialogue going on inside our heads, but others in the room will have no idea. Finding a way to have a presence, without leaving yourself feeling like a fish out of water, will help you to create a positive impression on those important stakeholders. Here are a few ideas to help you have the greatest impact when face-to-face with your stakeholders.

Avoid the temptation to quickly take a seat before a meeting starts. Instead of quietly sitting down and patiently waiting for the meeting to begin, use the time to assess the situation, the room, and those within it. Take a moment to think through some key questions:

- Why am I here?

- What do I need to take care of to get the most value from my time here?

- What do I want to do now to increase my presence?

- Who do I want to actively greet and engage with?

Once you are clear on these questions, use this time before the session starts to lay some important foundation stones. Identify the important stakeholders in the room. Make the effort to greet them and introduce yourself to anyone you don't know. I know that this can feel awkward and uncomfortable. A quiet 'Hi' or timid smile may not land, but 'Hi Mo. Great to see you. I'm looking forward to your presentation!' will instantly connect you with the presenter. Put the work in before the meeting starts and this will make it feel easier to engage during the rest of the session, asking questions or adding to the discussion more confidently.

Think about where you want to sit in the room. In my experience, there are two ideal spots to choose from.

The first is the high-traffic spot. This can be next to the door or near the coffee station in the meeting room. By stationing yourself here you can be sure to catch everyone as they are coming in and moving through the space. Just watch out that you are not having to constantly adjust your seat to let people through as you will end up feeling in the way. The second is the eye-line seat. This can be close to the presenter or in the line-of-sight between important stakeholders. This gives you the maximum opportunity to get into the conversation as you will be much more visible to people and they will more easily spot that you are trying to make a point, meaning less chance of being talked over, plus they are more likely to look to you for your point, even inviting your contributions.

If you are the one presenting, always stand up if you can and position yourself at the front of the room. It is becoming more common to adopt an informal presentation manner where everyone sits, and the style is more discursive. The risk in this for an introvert is that you can lose control of the session as bigger and louder voices chime in and eventually take over. Where possible, standing to speak gives you two advantages. It helps you to retain a calm composure by feeling grounded and opens your chest to breathe deeply, managing any anxiety and lowering stress levels. It also commands attention: people's eyes will be drawn to you, and they will look to you for direction, thereby helping you to stay in control of the session.

The same principles apply in the online setting, and I've seen many introverts thrive in streamed meetings in ways that they did not feel comfortable to do in person. Invest in a standing desk, laptop stand, or even a pile of books to enable you to stand up or sit up tall even in online meetings. Use the online chat feature or your company's messenger app to engage with the group or individuals before and during online sessions. Take the opportunity to write a short message or pose a succinct question in the chat box before the meeting starts and then follow this up with further thoughts in the live discussion. This can be a great way to share your point without having to struggle to find a space or interrupting. It also enables you to mull on something and contribute when you are ready, even after the topic has moved on, and to garner support for your idea alongside the presentation.

Getting buy-in from others

As introverts we typically enjoy solo work. In most roles we can only go so far alone, at some point we will need the input or sign-off of others. In achieving this, I have found that there are two important skills to bring to the forefront here: storytelling and connection.

Storytelling in business holds immense value and impact. Stories capture attention, making information seem more digestible and engaging. They humanise business and forge emotional connections with stakeholders by sharing a relatable context. Effective storytelling can simplify complex ideas and leaves a lasting impression.

At first glance, storytelling might seem like the strength of bold extraverts, but let's look at what is needed here as many of the qualities lie firmly within your introvert skillset. You can use your keen observational and attentive listening skills to capture nuanced details and emotions, enriching your narratives. Your deep thinking and thoughtful reflection skills will help you to deliver well-crafted and impactful stories. Your preference for deeper connections translates into authentic and genuine storytelling, fostering stronger emotional bonds with your audience, plus your excellence in one-to-one communication enables you to create personalised and compelling narratives tailored to specific people. These skills are some of our superpowers so let's put them to work.

Key to getting successful buy-in from others is the ability to build connection. Luckily, this plays strongly to your advantage. As introverts, we typically prefer deeper connections formed one-to-one or with a few people at a time. While big meetings, presentations, and workshops might be the flavour of the day in many companies, I do sometimes question the value of all those people sitting together for hours. There is certainly a time and a place for these group meetings, and we have already considered how you can lead and run these types of events successfully, but imagine the added depth of insight, ideas, and buy-in that can be achieved when you are able to connect with people in alignment with your superpower.

Here are some tips to connect with people in a way that has felt authentic to me as an introvert. First, plan out who you need to get on board with your project. You will need a range of different types of people. Think about who can give you great input, who can give you solid feedback, who will play devil's advocate, who will finance it, who can help you with the stuff you're not so good at doing, and from whom you will need a green light to advance. Is there anything missing from this list for your project?

At first it might seem like a lot of work to put time in the diary with each of these people individually. However, just twenty to thirty minutes with each will give you the one-to-one setting and the time for the deep conversations in which you thrive and, in my experience, you'll get more quality output working in this way than by sticking everyone in a huge room for hours.

Another tip to think about is putting people into a duo or trio to meet with you. This is probably still quite comfortable for you as it's a small group but still enables you to use your time more efficiently. There are also additional benefits as you will find that you can get them to spark off each other to generate fresh new ideas and they'll enjoy doing something different. That sounds like real impact, and a real win for the introvert way.

Also think about who influences who, and how to use a domino effect to spread your influence yet further – effectively, get your solid connections to do the work for you. The decision makers are more likely to buy in if they know others have too: 'I've already got great buy-in from Sales and from Finance. I'd love to get your input on two key points before I'm ready to fully pitch to you.' You have sparked their interest and made clear that you're genuinely interested in their input, while also sharing that other key stakeholders are engaged and on board. You've also set up an opportunity to test the waters with them before having to do the final presentation.

To get true buy-in from others, you must listen just as much as talk. Your impressive listening skills in one-to-one and small group situations will be invaluable to help you finesse your approach and prepare for future interactions. Listen for their needs and concerns so that you can consciously address them, not steamroller them as they might be used to in other settings. Pick up on what they get excited about and play back that language to reinforce it. Echo their words back in your other discussions so that all your stakeholders have the same vocabulary about your idea and project. This reinforces both clarity and connection across the group.

Sharing your successes

In most work environments, doing what you say you will and hitting your targets is only half the battle. To really thrive, you also need to put work in to ensuring that you get seen for the impact you're having. To achieve this, it is key to talk about your work with others and ensure that you are recognised for what you have achieved, otherwise your quieter and more subtle nature means your success could go unnoticed. This may feel uncomfortable and like showing off, but the reality is that if you don't put some attention into managing how your efforts are being seen, they won't be noticed next to those of your louder colleagues.

We want to shift the leadership statements from 'the category performed really well last quarter' to 'Jane drove a fantastic performance for the category.' It is important for an introvert to find an authentic way to achieve this so that it doesn't feel like boasting or standing awkwardly in the limelight, but credit where credit is due – own it. Whereas some extraverts will get out their megaphone whenever possible, your approach could be through 'micro-messages'. At every opportunity with your boss, with peers, with stakeholders, and with the stakeholders' assistants, have a ten-second message ready to inform people about what you are doing and the impact you are having. Some introverts may naturally default to talking about 'we' and 'the team', and there is absolutely a place for that, but first let's get *you* known for *your* impact.

These kinds of micro-messages are great to have up your sleeve so have a think about what this ten-second micro-message might look like. Keep it short and consider starting with a question as that will prompt the other person to ask you something back so that you can give more detail. Remember to keep the focus on what you have achieved: 'Did you know October was the highest selling month? That project I launched is really paying off.' 'Remember that new idea I pitched to you? It gained 10% more customers last month.' You have worked hard for these successes, so it is your right – and your responsibility – to ensure everybody knows.

Managing conflict

How to manage conflict and disagreement will vary depending on the specific situation and your unique introvert fingerprint. In my experience, introverts typically like, and look for, harmony between people and are often therefore fantastic peacekeepers, but it is important to watch out to ensure you don't put peace and harmony before your own needs and boundaries. If everyone else is happy at your expense, it is not sustainable, you are not thriving, and this is not OK. Managing conflict does not mean giving in – you can be assertive and still stay true to your introvert nature.

Although you may feel uncomfortable when faced with conflict, your introvert superpowers can really help you manage it. Now is the moment to use your skills to slow the situation down. Take as long as necessary to listen to all points of view and play back what you have heard without judgement. For example, 'What I'm hearing is...', 'How I'm feeling in this is...', and 'What I need in this situation is...'. Bring to the table your ability to analyse the situation and assimilate the facts to help make sense of the problem and to propose evidence-based alternatives. Share your enhanced understanding of the impact on the people this affects and propose ways to resolve it through dialogue and collaboration.

As introverts, we can often experience conflict painfully and personally, but remember that debate and challenge can be really healthy and can enable growth, both for the business and for individuals. It's usually the tone of the dialogue or uncontrolled and overflowing emotions that turn discussion and deliberation into a more negative conflict, so use your cool, calm nature to help yourself and others navigate through it.

To end this chapter, I feel it's important to think about how to take care of yourself when you are working on things that are challenging and feel uncomfortable, but despite your best efforts, don't go well.

Taking care of yourself after setbacks

When we've tried hard to stretch ourselves and been brave enough to try new things, it won't always work out first time. We are often quick to blame ourselves when things have not gone well and may feel like we never want to try this ever again. Remember that everyone has been here at some point – probably several times – but it will get better. Don't give up on yourself. You can, and you will, succeed, but to do this, you have to keep going.

Unfortunately shit happens. It's a fact. Perhaps our performance didn't go to plan, or life happened in an unexpected way. First thing is just to stop and take a breath. Step back from any ensuing drama and make sense of what's happened.

Here are some great questions to help to disentangle what was down to you and what was a result of the context surrounding you:

- What really happened?

- What is/was in my control?

- What can I learn/take from this to impact next time and help me with the way forwards?

Most people, and certainly the ones that matter, want you to succeed and will support you. Ask them for some objective and constructive feedback on how they saw the situation. What did they see you do well? What did they observe in you *and* in the context when things weren't going so well? Finally, discuss with them what you could learn from this. What should you keep doing next time (this is especially valuable if you have been trying out something new), and what should you stop doing or adjust.

Having worked through your reflection, take a rest. Too often we move straight from one battle and on to the next, despite feeling frustrated and frazzled. If you can, plan your diary to give you a proper break after a big event. If it's really not possible, make sure your evening or the next day is as clear as possible for you to do what you need to recover and recharge. The longer you leave it, the longer it will take to get back to where you need to be to deliver for whatever is coming up next.

When we are really depleted, the first step is self-soothing. After long periods of high-intensity stretch, before I could even consider thinking about re-energising, first I just needed to vegetate. Sometimes this phase gets called the 'introvert hangover'. You may have spent so much time in an extraverted environment, your attempts to try out new behaviours have drained you, and your battery has started running too low. In my earlier career I used to wonder what was happening to me when I felt so zapped of energy – was I depressed, burnt out, sick…? No, just an introvert with an energy hangover. It is more than OK to self-soothe to get yourself back to a point where you can actively refill your battery again. The key is to find a way to move forwards re-energised.

Self-soothing can take many forms and again, it will vary person to person. It may like look like a 'blanket burrito', a Netflix binge, or enjoying your favourite tipple… Its purpose is to take you right out and away from the stressor, allowing you to calm your system. Taking this time will help you to reset and begin recharging.

Be aware, however, that staying in self-soothing mode means remaining in a low energy state, effectively wallowing with a risk of slipping into a low mood and even self-sabotage. This sees a blanket burrito becoming a duvet day(s), series bingeing becoming 'just one more' into the early hours of the morning, and a glass of wine becoming an actual hangover. That's not being in control; that's allowing the situation to take over and is not going to get us to where we want to be.

To counter this, we soothe ourselves and then boost our energy with a positive action. For example, a blanket burrito morphs into some stretching on the couch or yoga, followed by a gentle walk or slow jog; Netflix bingeing shifts to motivational TED Talks or inspirational podcasts; a glass of wine evolves to a call with a close friend, or a community activity.

Even when things have gone brilliantly well, performing under stress needs to be followed by rest. Go ahead and celebrate your achievement, in whatever way is meaningful for you. Be aware that the buzz and adrenaline of success sometimes masks the low battery that is underneath. Asking yourself, 'How do I feel?', followed by prompting 'And what else?' repeated three times, can help you to assess the true situation under the surface. This is invaluable if you are to prevent a run of successes feeding a gradually building burnout.

Whatever happens, put yourself first. Be kind to yourself. Seek support from your colleagues, your friends, or a coach. You only stumble if you try, and that is a win in itself. Recognise and celebrate what you have achieved in using your superpowers and building new muscles in areas of your career that you have previously struggled with. Keep practising and you will thrive.

QUESTIONS FOR REFLECTION

Take a few moments to think about the following questions in relation to the challenging situations and interactions we have covered:

- In which two or three areas do you want to focus on building confidence and capability?
- Where can your introvert fingerprint and superpowers serve you?
- What are your go-to self-soothers? How can they shift to become positive boosters?
- What is your action plan to build this muscle in the next week, month, or three months?
- Who can support you in this journey?
- How will you measure and reward your success?

Thinking about these questions will help you find ways to remain authentic to yourself while also using your introvert superpowers to their maximum extent, benefiting you and others.

SIX

Leading Teams As An Authentic Introvert

'I will not follow where the path may lead, but I will go where there is no path, and I will leave a trail.'
— Muriel Strode

I f our preference is for quiet, solitary, reflective time, you might wonder how we can possibly hope to lead a group of other people effectively. This is a question I have been regularly asked. I remember it feeling horribly scary at first, with all eyes on me – my worst fear is being the centre of attention – waiting for direction, support, answers, and motivation. With a bit of thought, I realised that I had useful skills and traits to offer my team, including considered decision making, active listening, strategic thinking, depth of knowledge, and calm demeanour – qualities which are all typical of introverts. There were plenty of challenges along the way to building my confidence and capabilities as a manager and leader, not least when teams were used to being managed by a quite different style of leadership. I can undoubtedly say, though, that I grew into a well-respected and effective leader by using my natural strengths and enjoying honing my new skills.

First, it's important to distinguish between a leader and a manager as the terms often get used interchangeably. A manager manages the input/output process of people's work against the company and team goals. A leader is someone who makes the team greater than the sum of its parts. This is the kind of phrase that used to make my introvert nature nervous, fearing that I needed to stand on stage and give a rallying speech. I can assure you that it's not the case. Introverts make amazing leaders when they stay true to themselves. This chapter will help you to find and unlock your authentic introvert leadership superpowers.

Many leaders in the professional world lead in a bold and forceful way. I am sure that we have all experienced these people at some time. This way of leading does have its merits. It can get tasks done quickly and in the way the leader wants, but it does not always get everyone's engagement, and results can suffer as a consequence. Over time, this and a lack of empathy or provision for alternative preferences for ways of working leads to frustration and reduced productivity.

To my mind, what distinguishes a stand-out leader from a mediocre one is the ability to help others thrive and to do this in a way that role models the value of doing so in your own unique style. It's key to keep top of your mind that to be an effective and authentic leader is to be consistent in your way of being – for me there is nothing authentic about switching and flipping in front of different people – and to have the ability to set up conditions that support every person in your team, whatever their individual preferences may be. My opinion is that if someone is a leader that expects everyone to work in a style just like theirs, then they are not yet a *true* leader, even if they are managing a team. What they have not yet undertaken is the vital and healthy work necessary if they are to become an authentic leader who puts the goal of a thriving team at the forefront of their approach *and* creates a safe environment for team members to ask for what they need to operate at their best.

How introverts make exceptional leaders

In my experience, the best leaders are those that demonstrate a blend of drive and empathy. These might seem like opposite qualities, but having the ability to focus on building a successful business through goals, structure, and facts while also understanding people's needs, emotions, and motivators is typical of many introverts. As we have discussed, everybody has a different mix of qualities and traits, but the intention here is to support introverts in recognising how their quiet strengths can support them in becoming effective leaders that deliver results and create strong teams.

Let's take a closer look at the three main qualities it takes to be an exceptional leader, and how, from my experience, the typical superpowers of an introvert can serve each of them; we will also identify some watchouts to take note of along the way.

The imagination to set an inspirational vision

I remember asking a senior leader within my organisation, 'What do you do if you're not sure on the vision?' He replied calmly and simply, 'It doesn't matter as long as you always know where you're going.' I was a bit taken aback, but it's true. There are of course many times in life when just getting started and figuring things out as you go along, while enjoying the voyage of discovery along the way, is exactly what is needed. When you are leading a team, however, it is important to set a clear picture of success and vision for the future to bring clarity and ensure consistency in your team.

Don't think that this vision needs to be a thunderbolt of inspiration. Use your introvert powers of listening, analysis, problem solving, and understanding of the impact on people to build this vision. Seek input from others but remember that it's easy to lose our bearings and be overly influenced by what others think. Hold true to your course and don't be tempted to shift direction too quickly. I encourage you to decide on some review points in the calendar ahead and clearly communicate these, and how you will evaluate success, with your team. This stops the endless distraction of questions about *what* everyone is supposed to be doing and instead allows you and the team to focus on the *how* of delivering against the vision.

Don't allow your vision to sit quietly on the shelf. Talk about it often. Be proud of it – remind your team, remind your stakeholders. Build an elevator pitch for the moment you need to communicate it clearly and succinctly when put on the spot. Practise it until you don't have to think about it.

Skill in helping your team and its members thrive in their work

For you to thrive, the team needs to thrive. In turn, this means ensuring that each person is set up with the conditions they need to help them thrive too. Your opportunity to achieve this starts with your initial one-to-ones and the first team meeting. Start by listening. Ask your team what they need, what they expect, what they are great at, and what their concerns are. Don't slip into rescuer mode and promise to deliver and solve everything for them. Sometimes just recognising their point of view and empathising, adult to adult, is enough. There is a real possibility that this may be the first time anyone has ever asked them this type of questions so listening to them and acknowledging what they say is often extremely meaningful to them. Set expectations about what you're going to do with the information they've shared to avoid frustrations down the line.

If this really is their first time encountering this new approach to leadership, it can be really disorientating for people. I've had an experience when my team members couldn't identify what they needed and how they wanted to work so they could thrive. They were so impacted by a previous leader who operated through 'command and control' that their ability to think about their own needs was diminished and some even felt suspicious initially about my radically different approach. Talking openly about their experiences and giving them time to adjust helped people to think about things from a different perspective and consider how to articulate their expectations and identify new possibilities. Change takes time, and different amounts of time for different people. Stick with it.

For this to be successful, it is key to explain to the person and to the team what you are doing and your rationale for doing it. You can't overcommunicate in these situations and it is important not to make assumptions about how the other person has understood what you have told them. Check in and ask them to clarify that what you intended to say has really landed in the right way. My preference was to have a one-to-one session with each individual first. This meant that I could take the time to really listen and hear them, gradually piecing together a picture of their experiences, thoughts, and views while also testing out some of my ideas. As my teams got bigger, however, this was not always possible. Sometimes you just have to go for it – if you wait for the perfect moment, you'll never get started.

Adopting a coaching style in these discussions can support you in having conversations about what matters to your team. This leadership approach means helping your team grow by asking questions rather than always telling, really listening to what is – and often what is not – said, nudging their thinking with positive challenges, and being there to support in the good times and the bad. Your aim is to help make everyone responsible for their own performance and encourage independent thinking. Coaching means treating your team like adults who know the way forwards but just need the time and space to think in a supportive environment.

You may need to employ different leadership styles at different times and with different people, according to the situation. In my experience, coaching is the optimum leadership style 80% of the time, but sometimes you do need to take a different approach. For example, in an emergency it is appropriate to dictate what needs to be done and how. Another example would be choosing to communicate and model the way things should be done when performance is low and technical capabilities are lacking, to achieve the high standards required.

It's important and valuable to spend time working to understand everyone's differences and their current realities. You will have people in your team who love to work in the same way you do, and others who prefer to work quite differently. Both are great for you as a leader, and you can leverage their diverse skills and preferences to strengthen your team. The highest performing teams that I have either worked in or led have had a mix of extraverts and introverts: people who love to quietly analyse data, those that focus on people first, individuals who drive decisions and actions forwards, and those who enjoy engaging groups to get involved. Supporting everyone to work in their own preferred style will have people playing to their strengths and filled with energy to deliver individually and as a team. This is a win-win situation.

Discuss with your HR team about opportunities to work with team coaches or to workshop tools like Insights Discovery that can help people to better understand themselves, each other, and the relationships within the team. Once you have a clear understanding of your team members' preferences, strengths, and passions, you have the opportunity to support them by pinpointing and crafting additional opportunities for them to shine and develop further. Foster their personal growth and motivate them to take the lead in areas where there might be existing gaps. Understanding the skill distribution will also support you to delegate activities that are not aligned with your own strengths.

Never overlook the importance of prioritising your own well-being. Introverts will often put the well-being of others before their own, especially in a leadership role when they may feel highly responsible for others. Remember the undeniably sound aircraft safety instruction: 'Put on your own oxygen mask first before assisting others.'

We looked extensively at how to manage your energy levels and recover from setbacks earlier in the book. Now consider how you can share these learnings with your team and foster discussions about the tools they may need or could use to take care of themselves and each other. You can actively use these conversations to model behaviour you wish to see in your team, for example by providing clear boundaries and guidelines for expected ways of working. This may involve mastering the art of tactfully saying 'no' or offering a conditional 'yes, if…' response to requests.

Don't expect to be able to be everything to everyone all of the time. I've seen many new leaders start off feeling like they must have all the answers and are failing if they aren't able to do everything with ease. Leadership is not about concealing your vulnerability: by consciously sharing with the team experiences that create psychological safety and support, you can build connection and trust, and show that you too are human. I really encourage you to find a mentor, coach, or trusted colleague to discuss your challenges and support you with finding your authentic leadership style when you are starting out as a leader for the first time or taking on a new leadership role.

Amplifying success: Celebrating and sharing achievements

Whether you are being recognised for personal or team success, stepping into the limelight and being the centre of attention is not something introverts tend to look forward to. I am sure that many of us would rather the on-stage trapdoor opened up beneath our feet rather than face the spotlight! Remember, however, that your absolute worst nightmare could be someone else's dream scenario – applause, speeches, photographs to record the moment, etc. As a leader, you should celebrate and share in ways that encompass the preferred methods of both introverts and extraverts, to ensure nobody feels disregarded or that they have missed out. Introverts might prefer subtle one-on-one or written acknowledgements. Extraverts, on the other hand, generally thrive in the limelight and may appreciate public praise or lively team gatherings. The art lies in blending these approaches to ensure that every team member feels appropriately acknowledged and thanked.

Feeling appreciated is not enough – a good leader will go a step further to ensure that each person is also fully recognised for their achievement by the wider team and by the people who will input into annual reviews or promotion decisions. This is especially true for the quieter people in your team who may prefer not to have the fanfare and therefore risk having their contribution overlooked. Make sure to communicate their achievements in the same platforms as everyone else, give them the opportunity to participate, and never make assumptions about their willingness or capability to be part of it. Reinforce the communication around people's achievements directly with the key stakeholders who need to be informed.

All of this might initially feel awkward and almost like boasting. My advice is to construct a handful of clear, factual statements that explain what you and your team have achieved, to have ready to share when the opportunity arises. In addition, look to engineer a few bigger moments in the diary across the year to celebrate and recognise your team with others. Doing this in a way that suits the preferences of your team members will be really motivating and highly appreciated by the group.

Leading teams through challenges

I don't want to rain on your parade, but I would now recommend that you take some time to consider how you are also going to drive success in the more challenging times that you will inevitably encounter. Moments when there is high pressure and strong critique from others can make the team feel highly uncertain and vulnerable. For many leaders, it can also lead to self-doubt and feelings of imposter syndrome. It is important that the team know that you always have their backs, so they can operate with less stress. In my experience, it is about treating your team like capable professionals and supporting them with challenging care. I like to think of it as being a 'loving boot' – a high-support, high-challenge approach.

All companies will experience challenges and go through difficult times. Your aim will be to build a team which is able to successfully navigate these tense and challenging moments and comes out with a stronger bond and respect for each other's capabilities. You need to be a leader who empathises while making space for people to be heard, and who will hold up a mirror to identify any limiting assumptions and behaviours that are present in the team, so you can tackle them. You want to help your people to help themselves, all growing stronger as you do so.

However well managed, these moments can be stressful. People tend to become less tolerant and accommodating when under pressure, stress levels will rise, and tempers can flare. Introvert leaders may naturally shy away from confrontation, so preparation is your ally here. Equip yourself with facts, use your calm demeanour to defuse tense situations, and always know your aim in any discussion. Adopting a coaching leadership style in your conversations towards both your team and your surrounding stakeholders can really help steady things, by enabling people to see the topic from different perspectives and to understand the views of others.

When coming out on the other side, it is tempting to just move on and leave the difficult times behind. I encourage you, instead, to reflect with the team on what happened, the impact it has had, and what you have learned collectively. Doing so helps everyone to acknowledge the situation happened and fully move forwards from whatever difficulties took place with a refreshed energy and carrying a lighter load. Use what you learned earlier in this book about your personal battery and energy management to ensure you have sufficient fuel to continue leading your team as it works through the challenge and out on the other side.

If all of this feels rather overwhelming, it's OK, I have been there too. I've had to manage that niggling voice telling me 'I can't...', making me doubt 'what if...?' and thinking heavily about the reaction of others. No one has all the right answers first time, and the good news is that you are not expected to either. Remember that you are not doing this alone, and that learning by doing is the best way to find your own authentic leadership style that brings you confidence and results.

If you are new to leadership, and even if this isn't your first rodeo, I recommend you do three things:

1. Be confident in asking for what you need from your line manager and from HR when stepping into your first or a new leadership role. It's tempting to feel that as the leader you cannot show weakness: don't fall into this trap. Weakness is not seeking support. True strength lies in recognising where your skills are best used and getting the right support to either delegate to others or seek training to fill the gaps.

2. Build a community of allies around you with different experiences and capabilities. Most people like to be asked to share their knowledge or experience and will be keen to help you. Think about who you already know, or who you can contact, that has skills or behaviours that you still want to grow as a leader.

3. Working with a mentor who you respect can be really beneficial when seeking specific guidance in new or challenging situations. A coach can be invaluable to support you in working through how you want to achieve your goals and in finding ways of developing your own authentic leadership style with confidence and energy.

Understanding yourself as a leader, with all your strengths and weaknesses, will help you to grow and support you in developing a team that works to the best of their abilities, both individually and collectively.

Moving on as a leader

As you progress in your career, at some stage you will need to hand over the leadership of your team to your successor. It's likely that your style of leadership will differ in some way from theirs and the transition can cause a shockwave (or at least a tremor) in your team. It is likely that they will have grown used to your supportive, coaching style of leadership, based on deep listening and professional care. Whoever succeeds you in taking the lead of your team, you can support everyone through the transition by preparing both the individual team members and the next manager. Use your one-to-one sessions to help your team think through what the impact of the change is likely to be and what they will need from the new manager. Without exposing any confidential information, also take every opportunity to share with the new manager what makes the team tick and what they will need to focus on to help the team continue to thrive going forwards.

In your journey of leading a thriving team, remember that it's not just about steering; it's about empowering your team members to navigate their own course while still being their biggest supporter. This is the essence of leadership – helping others to flourish, and in doing so, creating a team that achieves greatness together.

QUESTIONS FOR REFLECTION

Reflect on your introvert fingerprint and what qualities you can bring to leadership:

- How do I want to define myself as a leader?
- What superpowers can I bring to leading a team?
- Where might I have skillset gaps that might challenge me in my leadership journey?
- What are the two or three priority areas that I would like to work on?
- What tools and support could I call on to help me?

SEVEN

The Future-Ready Introvert: Role Modelling Leadership Behaviours

'The best transformation leaders we have worked
with all share one powerful trait: the ability and
discipline to step back, to reflect and to then focus
their leadership energy in the right places at the
right time.'
— Tim Clayton-Ball and Euan Isles, Deloitte

Before you begin this chapter, I invite you to have a
go at what Tim Clayton-Ball and Euan Isles identify as critical in any attempt at leading transformation:
step back, reflect and refocus. Take a moment to think
about the future: your future, the future of your company, the future of those around you and the planet
we collectively call 'home'. What are your hopes for
that future? What does it look like in your wildest
dreams? What are your fears and the watchouts to

pay attention to? Keep a note of the themes that have come up for you. We will come back to those later in the chapter.

The world of work is changing, just as the world itself continuously evolves every day. We cannot accurately predict the future, but we can put ourselves in a position to better understand what it might be and what our role within it could be. Topics for us to think about include how and where we might work, the best approach to address complex issues around growth, technology, and climate/regeneration, and the leadership behaviours that will be required to navigate all of this.

In researching this chapter, I read several reports on the future of work published over the last few years by notable consultants and big consulting firms to see what common conclusions we can draw to help us navigate what will be important in the future and how we can be part of (leading) that change. I was expecting to be overwhelmed by a tech fascination with the rise of AI, and machines increasingly taking over routine tasks. This was certainly in there, but to a far lesser extent than I had anticipated, and instead they were dominated by some themes that I found really inspiring. These included human-centric leadership (a prioritisation of people and culture), the importance of connection, and the value of inclusion. They set out a future in which the alpha 'command and control' style of leadership is defunct. In its place is a new type of leader who takes the time to listen to others, to reflect on the way forwards, and who maintains an ongoing virtuous cycle of acting and continuously reviewing to keep things on course towards a meaningful vision.

I think introverts have a really important role to play in this future. Your unique introvert superpowers are hugely aligned with the needs of corporations and teams in navigating the way forwards. Leadership in the future will require you to maintain a careful balance between your powerful introvert qualities and your trained 'extravert-muscles' to impact people across your organisation, knowing when to dial up or down particular characteristics in your approach. This isn't shapeshifting or pretending to be someone you are not; it is about knowing your audience and adapting your approach to resonate with their needs.

How, then, can we become a future-ready introvert in the world of work? Let's look at three key areas:

- How and where we work
- Addressing increasingly complex issues
- New leadership styles and behaviours

How and where we work

Technology is changing the way we work. We see this already on a daily basis. It was apparent before the COVID-19 pandemic, and growing trends such as remote working and virtual meetings only accelerated during lockdown. Organisations are now trying to determine new rules and guidelines for hybrid working or returning full-time to the office. I encourage you to think about the office as a tool to support your work and career rather than as a destination itself. Just as Zoom, Messenger, or any other communication platform are tools to aid working, so you can start to think of the office as just another communication platform available to use when appropriate.

As we've learned, there are some things that can be done successfully in a virtual setting. These are primarily situations in which proximity is not so important, such as when sharing information, reaching final decisions, or co-ordinating work. However, for this to happen most effectively in the virtual world requires trust. Trust within the team works like the glue and the grease in the system. It binds you together as a strong unit and gets you through those difficult situations and challenging periods as one cohesive whole.

In my experience, I find trust is still best built face-to-face and gradually. It's often in those 'in-between' moments where the real sharing and relationship building occurs: in the breaks between agenda items, in between two meetings, in the walk between the office and the car park, and so on. These small moments allow you to show your more personal side, to share common experiences, or just to be a listening ear. In my experience, it's also in those in-between moments that introverts can often really thrive. I'm not talking about awkward small talk, but about those introvert superpower moments when the pressure is off, you have the space to think, and the time to listen deeply to someone.

Your approach to this could be a real game changer in terms of how and where people work. It might also begin to tackle the conundrum vexing execs the world over: how to stem the increasing problems of 'quiet quitting' (employees reducing their output and effort to the bare minimum without formally resigning), gradual disengagement, and lack of connection among their workers.

It doesn't have to be a binary choice between home or office, of course. Think creatively and there are plenty of ways of spending time with colleagues, in person but outside the office. It can be a walk outdoors as a team, or it could be meeting at an offsite location close to where your colleagues live, such as an art gallery or museum – get imaginative with the location. This is a really nice way to build trust with people, to share your interests, and discuss things outside of work (even if you draw the line at sharing the intricacies of your personal life!). Think about what you need to have these moments with your colleagues. What does your team need and how can you create the best environment for that to happen?

Addressing increasingly complex issues

Inclusion and equity for all people, including all personality types, is fundamental if we are to begin to solve the complex problems of our time. Diversity brings richness to the problem-solving process, ensuring that a broader spectrum of ideas, experiences, and talents can be included. Taking an inclusive approach and embracing all contributions enhances the overall decision-making process by ensuring that any decisions will have first considered all potential consequences and implications. In a rapidly changing world, characterised by constant uncertainty and challenges, adaptability becomes a key strength. When we put in place a diverse team made up of individuals with varied characteristics, we contribute to increased versatility, enabling the group to navigate problems with agility and easily embrace new perspectives and change. Fostering an inclusive environment also brings increased employee engagement, where individuals feel valued and will contribute their best efforts towards working together towards a common goal.

Everyone has a vital role to play in this. While there is an increasing urgency for action, this needs to be balanced with strategic thoughtfulness and considered planning to ensure that the right actions are taken with a clear understanding of the goals, potential challenges, and long-term implications. This balance allows for effective decision making and the implementation of actions that align with overarching objectives, simultaneously fostering both efficiency and effectiveness. It is natural for everyone to feel anxious, perhaps even overwhelmed, by the enormity of some of the global challenges facing us at the moment. Remember that you are not alone in this, and by working together, we can start to initiate some real change. I invite you to bring your acute listening skills, curiosity, and thirst for knowledge to play as you deep dive into diverse perspectives and actively work to bring in every voice and make it count. Your approach can make the difference.

New leadership styles and behaviours

AI offers the opportunity to free us from routine and repetitive tasks. This means that those of us with skills in more complex and cerebral tasks, including problem solving, leadership, empathy, and creativity will be increasingly highly valued by companies and the people within them. This future requires a shift in leadership skills from the more traditional 'command and control' style to something more focused on the individual – more human-centric. Human-centric leadership focuses on putting people at the forefront of decision making and organisational strategy. It emphasises empathy, collaboration, and a deep understanding of the needs, aspirations, and well-being of individuals within the organisation. Leaders following this approach prioritise creating a positive and inclusive work culture, fostering strong relationships, and recognising the unique strengths of each team member. My hope for human-centric leadership is that it brings a fresh focus to finding purpose, engagement, happiness, and well-being as individuals, while supporting the (re)growth of people, company, and nature.

Overall, the emphasis on people, empathy, and collaboration in human-centric leadership makes this style well-suited for introverts who often thrive in environments that value meaningful connections, deep understanding, and thoughtful leadership. Introverted leaders are great at creating environments where team members feel heard, valued, and appreciated. Our preference for deep, thoughtful interactions helps us to understand the unique strengths and aspirations of individuals, contributing to a workplace culture that prioritises inclusivity and personal growth. I also see that an introvert's natural inclination towards strategic decision making aligns well with the human-centric approach, ensuring that leadership actions not only address immediate needs but also consider the long-term well-being and success of both individuals and the organisation.

If we are to reframe the way we lead, we also need to look again at how we assess success and how we talk about failure. Existing measures are becoming less and less meaningful. Metrics such as year-on-year volume and financial growth or return for shareholders now begin to feel less relevant when considered in light of the reality of the global situation. To be effective in focusing on what matters, we need to broaden our conception of success. What are the most impactful ways to build points of reference beyond the traditional measures for us and for our teams? These need to be focused on people, inclusivity, and well-being, and the planet, sustainability, and regeneration of nature. It can be our role to connect deeply with others, to ensure everyone understands the need for this fundamental shift in values.

Imagine what the future could look like if everybody worked together in this way? As the nature of work evolves into the 'next normal' phase, everyone has an opportunity to demonstrate, and even change, what that could be. This has to be done in an authentic, genuine, and efficient way. As introverts, we know how exhausting it can be wasting huge amounts of energy trying to figure out how to *be* at work and striving to meet an extravert benchmark of what 'good' looks like. When researching this book, I spoke to so many introverts who told me that they wish someone had said to them earlier in their career that 'it's OK to be you,' and that 'you can do it your way; you don't have to fake it.' This is your opportunity to do just that – to live and breathe your authentic way and to role model it for others.

I also had many people saying that they have either not really thought about how the work environment generally favours the natural approach of extraverts, or how the prevailing behaviour perpetuates it. Together, whatever our role or level of seniority, we all have a role to ensure our working worlds include everyone's voice and contributions, to support everyone to thrive. The future of our careers – as well as our planet – depends on it.

QUESTIONS FOR REFLECTION

Take a look at the list of hopes, dreams, fears, and watchouts that you noted at the beginning of this chapter, and then consider the following questions:

- What do you think as you look at these now?
- Which of these are you drawn to act upon?
- What do you already have within your unique fingerprint of introvert superpowers to bring to the table, and how can you use these to make the difference to the future of work for yourself and those around you?
- Note down two or three actions that you want to take to ensure you are future ready and contributing to the difference you want to see in the world.
- What do you need to do first to get started on this journey? Who or what can support you?

Conclusion: Putting Your Ideas Into Action

'Success is never final; failure is never fatal.
It's courage to continue that counts.'
— Winston Churchill

A s you reach the final pages of this book, I'd like you to take a moment to remind yourself why you first picked up this book. Whether it was about learning something new, getting a different perspective, or perhaps to make a positive change in your working life, I hope you now have several ideas to put into action.

I really hope that learning about my experiences and trying out some of my suggestions will help you in finding your own way of being successful as an introvert in your career. I honestly believe that the unique qualities and superpowers that you identified in your introvert fingerprint can lead to huge success and personal fulfil-ment in your career, particularly now you know how and when to employ them to achieve maximum impact.

Finding the balance between using your introvert superpowers to their full potential and finding new ways to enjoy building muscles for skills that don't typically come naturally is challenging – otherwise you would not have needed this book! It takes courage to try and time to build confidence. Keep going – you are not alone, and I am proof that you can do it. Now it's your turn to discover your authentic way to thrive and to become a role model for fellow introverts everywhere.

QUESTIONS FOR REFLECTION

Reflect on what you have read in this book and look back through the notes you have made in the previous exercises, before answering the following questions:

- What have you learned about yourself and how will you use this in your career?

- Has your view on being an introvert changed? What does thriving as an introvert mean to you now?

- What are the key points that you are taking away and actions you are committing to?

- What do you commit to doing in the next week, month, three months, and beyond?

- What support do you need to put in place to help you get there?

> • What do you want to share with others about
> your experiences of being an introvert and reading
> this book?

I'd like to offer you a few final thoughts to close the book:

- **Embrace your uniqueness:** Your introvert qualities are not a limitation or a hindrance, they are your superpowers. Embrace your uniqueness and the value you bring to the table. Your perspective is not just valuable, it's indispensable.

- **Self-discovery is ongoing:** The journey to understanding yourself as an introvert is an ongoing process. Keep exploring, keep learning, and keep growing. You'll continue to uncover new facets of your introvert strengths throughout your life. Enjoy the process and celebrate each new discovery. Your potential is endless.

- **Confidence is a skill:** Confidence is not a static trait; it's a skill that can be developed. Practise self-affirmation, recognise your achievements, and celebrate your growth. You are more than capable of achieving remarkable things.

- **Employ effective energy management:** As an introvert, managing your energy is vital. Your reserves are not limitless, and in some areas of professional life, you will expend more energy than others might. Effective energy management is an art but one that is one well within your capabilities. Learn to recognise when you need to recharge and when you can give your all. This balance is essential for sustained success.

- **Authenticity is your greatest asset:** Authenticity is magnetic. Be true to yourself, and you'll attract genuine connections and opportunities. You don't need to fake it 'til you make it; you can thrive just by being you.

- **You're a champion for introvert success:** As you move forwards, remember that you're not just paving the way for yourself but for a large community of introverts. Be a champion for introvert success. Become the inspiration you needed, and support others on their journeys.

Thank you for embarking on this journey with me. Your commitment to personal and professional growth is commendable. As you move forwards, remember that you have a wealth of strengths, strategies, and support at your disposal.

Your future as a thriving introvert in your career is bright, and it begins now. Embrace it and make it uniquely yours.

With warmest wishes for your success,

Sarah

Bibliography

Abrahams, M, *Think Faster Talk Smarter: How to speak successfully when you are put on the spot* (S&S/Simon Element, 2023)

Angelou, M, *Letter to My Daughter* (Random House, 2009)

Baker, C, *Ernest Hemingway Selected Letters 1917–1961* (Simon and Schuster, 2003)

Cain, S, *Quiet: The power of introverts in a world that can't stop talking* (Penguin, 2013)

Cheek, JM, Brown, CA and Grimes, JO, *Personality Scales for Four Domains of Introversion: Social, thinking, anxious, and restrained introversion. Preliminary*

Research Manual, 2nd ed (Department of Psychology, Wellesley College, Wellesley MA, 2014)

Clayton-Ball, T and Isles, E, 'Time to Transform: Part 2 – Creating the conditions for successful change' (Deloitte, 30 June 2023), www.deloitte.com/uk/en/blog/future-of-work/2023/time-to-transform-2.html, accessed January 2024

Clear, J, *Atomic Habits: An easy and proven way to build good habits and break bad ones* (Random House, 2018)

Houston, E, 'Introvert vs extravert: A look at the spectrum and psychology', PositivePsychology.com (9 April 2019), https://positivepsychology.com/introversion-extraversion-spectrum, accessed March 2024

Meyer, E, *The Culture Map: Decoding how people think, lead, and get things done across cultures* (PublicAffairs, 2014)

Ong, SA, *Energize: Make the most of every moment* (Penguin Business, 2022)

Watts, G and Morgan, K, *The Coach's Casebook: Mastering the twelve traits that trap us* (Inspect & Adapt Ltd, 2015)

Acknowledgements

A special mention to my family who supported, encouraged, and championed me with curious questions and a belief in me that I never expected. You helped me to trust that this book could become a reality, and without you, this book would never have been finished.

For my dear 'Brum Fun' friends who I have known since our teenage years when I thrived at being awkward, thank you for being you and for always having nothing but kindness and love to offer, come rain or shine. You are an incredibly special group of people: Hannah, Jenny, Claire, Kath, Clare, Dave.

I'm grateful for the unwavering support and excitement for this project from my brilliant peer coach,

Jayne, who helped me put on my big girl pants on more than one occasion and encouraged me to just go for it. Similarly, Magda and Magriet, who have seen so much of my introvert journey at work and helped me to feel confident in setting up The Quiet Catalyst.

Thank you to the team at The Published Expert – Shaa, Matt, Stephanie, and Teara – who supported me in moving from scattered ideas to an actual manuscript. It was exactly the know-how and structure that I needed to get this book written. I am grateful to my writing buddies – Roz, Narinder, Susan, and Emma – for riding the writing rollercoaster with me and for being so open about the good, the bad, and the ugly throughout. Thank you also to Ruth from Optimus Coach Academy for the great Mastermind session to share your guidance as a published author.

I also want to mention and thank my first writing teacher, Talia, who helped me to feel confident about being creative and sharing it with others. Also, a mention of thanks to Claire, the creatrix who helped me to get started on the idea for this book, sitting in the fresh air surrounded by piles of sticky notes. Anytime I get stuck with my writing I go back to that place. Thank you both.

The team at Rethink Press – Sarah, Anke, Kathy, Hannah, Jez, Lucy, Joe, and Sophie – have been a joy to work with, and I am grateful for all their support to turn my manuscript into a published book.

Finally, saving the best for last, Gavin, my partner. He has been so patient and my ultimate cheerleader throughout this process. He has listened to my self-scathing diatribe on bad days and tolerated my enthusiastic energy for everything on the fortunately more numerous good days. His boosts of positivity all along the way, from initial idea to publication, have kept me going when it would have been so easy to give in and stop. Thank you x

The Author

 Sarah Manley, a seasoned professional with two decades of international experience in prominent corporate organisations across the UK and the Netherlands, brings a wealth of expertise to her role as a life and career coach, consultant, and author. Armed with a unique academic background, encompassing a degree in Human and Physical Geography from Durham University and a postgraduate degree in Marketing from Birmingham University, Sarah initially embarked on a trajectory within the medical devices sector, ultimately expanding her influence into the broader realms of healthcare, personal health, and medical nutrition.

Embracing change as an opportunity, a pivotal redundancy became the catalyst for Sarah's transformative journey. Her optimistic and compassionate approach to guiding others is rooted in a genuine passion for learning, and for supporting individuals on their unique paths. As an introvert, Sarah draws upon her own experiences to illuminate the way for others. Her business, The Quiet Catalyst, not only reflects her coaching and consultancy services, but also stands as a testament to her journey as an introverted professional. It serves as a platform for her supportive and knowledgeable voice, offering valuable insights to others navigating the corporate landscape.

Beyond her professional endeavours, Sarah is an advocate for sustainability and regenerative solutions for the planet. Her commitment to an active lifestyle is evident through her love of hiking, running, and yoga, balanced by the joy of immersing herself in the pages of a captivating book, preferably under a cosy blanket. With a blend of professional acumen and a genuine curiosity about life, Sarah's work resonates with wisdom, growth, and a deep understanding of what it means to be a quiet person.

🌐 www.thequietcatalyst.com

in http://linkedin.com/in/sarahmanleytqc

⊙ @thequietcatalyst